TO JAMES MARTINEZ

[signature]
4.14.14

To share in the world of Frank Lloyd Wright was to be immersed in the spirit of architecture as a sacred trust between our human pursuits and the gifts of the Creation which he saw as being the body of God. When he counseled his apprentices to "learn from the one great book of Nature," he was referring to the essential qualities of a sustainably beautiful way of life. And in his last year when he said, "I'll probably die with my work half done," he was referring to something far more holistic than designing for an ever-greater array of houses and buildings. What follows has grown from the seeds he both planted and nourished by his mentoring life and work.

FRANK LLOYD WRIGHT'S UNFINISHED WORK

It is time to sort out Earth and calculate what it will take to provide a satisfying and sustainable life for everyone into the indefinite future. The question of the century is: How best can we shift to a culture of performance, both for ourselves and for the biosphere, that sustains us?

–E.O. Wilson
Pulitzer Prize-winning biologist

Vernon D. Swaback, FAIA, FAICP

**Two Worlds
Community Foundation**

7550 East McDonald Drive . Suite A
Scottsdale, Arizona 85250
info@twoworldsfoundation.org
www.twoworldsfoundation.org
Telephone 480.991.1942

Book cover and layout by Pao Cagnina

ISBN 978-0-615-93343-6

With appreciation to Buckminster Fuller who liberated
and integrated our way of thinking by connecting
everyday life to the wonders of science and technology.
And to Frank Lloyd Wright who expanded our
understanding of beauty by connecting what we build
and how we live to the high performance examples and
lessons of nature.

To Vernon Swaback
With many rich memories of
various meetings put particularly
our meeting here at Talesin West
in Praul's last year--how wonderful
and loving a meeting it of was.
Buckminster Fuller

June 8 1968

CONTENTS

Foreword 2

Introduction 5

Designing the Future 8

Economics, Science, Art, and Religion 19

From Plato to the Present 32

Utopia or Oblivion........................ 36

Technology and Its Limits........................ 45

Ownership and Stewardship 51

The Anatomy of Peace 58

Frank Lloyd Wright's Unfinished Work 73

The United Children of Earth 97

Surrounded by Miracles........................ 119

The Creative Community........................ 131

Frank Lloyd Wright Center for the Future.............. 138

Afterword 147

Putting it all Together........................ 151

Notes........................ 159

Bibliography........................ 164

Index........................ 174

FOREWORD

Frederick Steiner, Ph.D.

Architects wake up each day dreaming about how to change the world for the better. Often, these are modest plans—a house remodel, a business addition. Architects undertake jobs for clients to, yes, make a living, but also to improve the places where people live and work. Sometimes, the medium is more ambitious—a place of worship, a school, a museum; places designed to lift the lives of a community. Frequently, architects become involved in plans for neighborhoods, cities, and regions. Every once and a while, an architect wakes up seeking to create a new world order. Vern Swaback is such an architect.

Swaback began his career on a lofty plane. An apprentice of Frank Lloyd Wright, Swaback was among members of the master's inner circle who completed their mentor's projects after his 1959 death. These projects included the Guggenheim Museum, the Marin County Government Center, Gammage Auditorium, and other notable commissions. From this beginning, Swaback went on to establish his own productive and consequential practice in Arizona. Like Wright, while grounded in architecture, Swaback has been active in many city-planning endeavors. Also like Wright, we have published his ideas, including this book about designing the world.

What does it take to design the future of our planet?
A purpose.
A vision.
A plan.
(and some humility)

The purpose is clear. The planet is filling up with a lot more of us. We have become an increasingly urban species. In the process, we use more energy and other resources. Important wildlife habitats and valuable farmland is disappearing. Meanwhile, the climate of the planet is heating up and natural disasters are increasing in frequency and in magnitude. We need designers to take on these challenges.

Swaback's vision builds on the ideas of Buckminster Fuller's ideas (among leading thinkers). Fuller advocated a"global perspective, a positive vision of the future and the means for achieving it." Concerning the means, Fuller possessed confidence in design, observing that "the best way to predict the future is to design it." For Swaback, such design should involve doing more with less. Nature provides a model for such efficiency.

To create a plan, Swaback advocates that humanity becomes our client. In the process, humanity becomes the architect. As Fuller observed, "On Spaceship Earth, there are no passengers, only crew." To become capable crew members, especially the young need to learn as much as possible about their spaceship.

And, about humility, certainly architects learn to be humble in working with their clients. Design involves ideas and options, iteration and amendment. Swaback, however, proposes another level of humility, one that suggests a new way of regarding the land. He recommends stewardship with ownership, which acknowledges the very real temporal limitations of each individual as well as our responsibility to pass on the world to future generations better than we inherited it.

Through this book, Swaback lays out a purpose, a vision, and a plan to design our world. He provides a blueprint for global design.

Mr. Steiner is the Dean of the School of Architecture and Henry M. Rockwell Chair in Architecture, The University of Texas at Austin. He has worked with local, state, and federal agencies on diverse environmental plans and designs. Dean Steiner was the second president of the National Academy of Environmental Design, the past president of the Hill Country Conservancy (a land trust), and past chair of Envision Central Texas (a non-governmental regional planning organization).

As a Fulbright-Hays scholar in 1980, he conducted research on ecological planning at the Wageningen University, The Netherlands. He was a 1998 Rome Prize Fellow and 2013-14 Resident at the American Academy in Rome. He is a Fellow of the American Society of Landscape Architects and was a visiting professor at Tsinghua University in Beijing, China (2005-2007). He received his Ph.D. and M.A. degrees in city and regional planning and a Master of Regional Planning from the University of Pennsylvania. He earned a Master of Community Planning and a B.S. in Design from the University of Cincinnati and an honorary M.Phil. in Human Ecology from the College of the Atlantic.

Dean Steiner has published numerous articles and books. His most recent books include Urban Ecological Design (with Danilo Palazzo, 2011), Design for a Vulnerable Planet (2011), Planning and Urban Design Standards (Student Edition with Kent Butler, 2007), The Essential Ian McHarg: Writings on Design and Nature (2006), and Human Ecology: Following Nature's Lead (2002).

INTRODUCTION

"We are called-upon to be architects of the future, not its victims."

–R. Buckminster Fuller

To live, work and study with Frank Lloyd Wright was to feel a timeless connection to both the past and future in which the divisions between, economics, science, religion, technology and art, seemed more like a single tapestry where, like nature, everything is interconnected and interdependent.

To experience Wright's genius at close range, was to be immersed in a continual flow of ideas in their most comprehensive, integrated and timeless sense. His definition of an idea was "salvation by imagination". At the center of it all was his intuitive sense and love of nature, which he thought of as being "the body of God". Now, we know more than ever before, that this gift of creation, that Wright so studied and revered, is under the assault of our growing human dominance. Wright's unfinished work is discussed more fully in its own chapter, but at its core, it is the urgent need to become more holistic in our thinking about a future that is each and every day more dependent on what we believe and commit to make happen. Living at a time of unprecedented, short-term distractions, made ever-more intrusive by instant everything, our journey begins with this summary of the present.

"Gaia (the earth) went its creative way for several billion years, becoming steadily more diverse, complex, and fruitful. Then, in the last few seconds of life's evolutionary day," *Homo sapiens* appeared – a creature that has wrought changes as great as several glaciations and other geological upheavals together, and has done it all within a flicker of the evolutionary eye. The evolution of *Homo sapiens* has produced a being that can think: a being that is aware, that can speculate about tomorrow, and can even plan for it.[1] We are the first species to become a geophysical force, single-handedly altering Earth's atmosphere and climate. We have initiated the sixth great extinction spasm of geological history by the massive destruction of ecosystems and the loss of plant and animal species." [2]

A significant, closer to home reality, is a world population that expands by a quarter of a million people each day resulting in shortages of agricultural land, fresh water and fossil energy. [3]

These and related insights call for a new and far more conscious approach to design including the relatedness and coordination of what our individual commitments and actions are adding up to becoming. At its most artful best this relatedness of all things is what Frank Lloyd Wright called *organic*, and legendary designers like Buckminster Fuller referred to as *synergy*, along with what Ian L. McHarg invented in the form of *ecological planning*. The work of Wright, Fuller, and McHarg was unique to their own way of seeing but all three would likely agree that "Beauty is our surest indication of whether or not what we do is in the most creative direction for nature as a whole." [4]

For anyone fascinated by the drama of big picture issues, the 21st century is a most amazing time to be a player, or at least a witness. We are living at a collision point between those who are profiting in ways that take a toll on the eco-system services of nature, others who are engaged in the accelerating focus on all things sustainable, and the latest version of still others who are placing their faith in the coming age of abundance by way of the ever-increasing reach of technology.

If we pull back just a bit from our more familiar metrics, we might easily agree that there are two sources of wealth – the ones that we create for ourselves, and the others that include the workings of nature, which created and continue to supply the resources of our planetary home. To expand the reach and understanding of design in the future, just as Wright did in the past, is nothing more than to accept

6

responsibility for the awesome power that has been placed within our grasp. It is a power that can either follow nature's example for doing more with less or to bring an extravagant end to humanity's brief time on earth.

We are living at a time of multiple transitions and for the first time in human history, both the cause and the impact of these transitions are all global. Because we are living at the dawn of the first global civilization, the most creative design-based insights will be those that propose possibilities that are far more integrated than anything known to the past. This way of seeing is what Frank Lloyd Wright referred to as "taking a positive hand in creation." The more we understand and broaden the reach of design, the more empowered we will become in our ability to provide for the yet-unborn who will either suffer or thrive as a result of what and how we plan for their arrival. For this way of seeing, we might easily imagine Wright announcing that, "the client is the future, the most significant programs will be those first conceived by visionary designers, and among the most important initiatives will be those for which there will be no one to send the invoice." Other dominant players who are daily diminishing or expanding our human potential are to be found within the realms of economics, science, religion and governance.

These various interests will always be with us, but moving closer to center stage is the very different world of design, specifically the disciplines of design that draw their inspiration from the holistic workings of the Creation. Nature is the gold standard of self-renewing abundance. Among the greatest insights for the future will be our awakening to the reality that beauty, rather than being a matter of style or taste, is the most convincing evidence of truth.

Long before I could have any idea as to what form it might take, I had a dream that I would one day be privileged to explore and work on something so essential that it would go beyond anything I could have started and would never be able to finish. The writing of this book, including the ideas and commitments of those whose lives it represents, are all part of that dream.

Vernon D. Swaback
Scottsdale, Arizona

DESIGNING THE FUTURE

"The secret of change is to focus all your energy not

on fighting the old, but on building the new."

–Socrates

The great architect Pietro Belluschi, described what he called *communal art,* "not as something produced by a few intellectuals or speculators but by the spontaneous and continuing activity of a whole people with a common heritage, acting under a community experience."[1] Another esteemed architect, Eero Saarinen, described his approach to design as a series of relationships in which he always considered whatever he was working on in terms of its next larger context. When designing a chair, he would, for example, consider it in relationship to the room in which it is to become a feature, and then the room related to the house followed by the house related to the neighborhood. Frank Lloyd Wright's version of this continuity was, "It is the relatedness of all things that creates value." And more specifically he insisted that, "It is quite impossible to consider the building as one thing, its furnishings as another, and its setting and environment, still another." It would seem inevitable that at some point, Belluschi's "communal art," Saarinen's, "next larger context" and Wright's "relatedness of all things" would have to embrace something far greater than what any one client could "commission."

On November 9, 1964 the Museum of Modern Art opened an exhibition under the banner, *Architecture without Architects*. It was billed as vernacular architecture that "does not go through fashion cycles." One that is nearly "unimprovable since it serves its purpose to perfection." [2]

Considering the exhibition's quite specific and extraordinary evidence of design and human achievement, a less catchy but more expressive title might have been, *An Architecture of Community*. Rather than a collection of stand-alone structures, the images were all those of symphonic, three-dimensional relationships, appearing inseparable from each other, and all together, from the land.

The structures were not only created from the earth, they were of the earth. And they were not only designed and constructed by the community, they expressed the idea of community. Everything was built with an integrated sense for its human use. And while these settlements were designed and constructed for a long-ago time, the lessons they expressed are timeless.

Contextual Artistry

Instead of the too-often artlessness of today's buildings that show little or no awareness of their context, these early developments were as coordinated and flowing as the land itself. Inasmuch as the builders had no choice but to work with both the environment and the materials at hand, they created in whole cloth the sustainability that we now address with the fragmentation of codes and ordinances, along with the marketing of "green" services, products, and systems that can be isolated and packaged for sale. It hasn't yet occurred to us, or perhaps it is for commercial reasons that we don't acknowledge that at least 75 percent of the performance-related issues associated with being *smart, green and sustainable* are more behavioral than technological. Furthermore, many of the patterns of behavior that matter most are formed at a very early age, and increasingly without any experiential and beneficial contact with nature. In addition to this deprivation of the young and old alike, another relates to our limited definition of art. We more easily associate the word and idea of "art", whether it hangs on a gallery wall, gets written in a book or performed on a stage, as something special and beyond the experiences of everyday life. This definition is fine as far as it goes, but for the 21st century, the definition of what we need most, starts where treating art as a specialty leaves off.

The MoMA "Architecture Without Architects," exhibition, was chronicled in an accompanying publication by Bernard Rudofsky, an architect, engineer and critic. Rudofsky made it clear that the only commonality of the collected works is that they all represented an architecture that transcends what any one client or even a group of clients could ever commission. It was as we have pointed out, an architecture of community.

In Rudofsky's words, the extraordinary range of large scale habitats were "produced not by specialists but by the spontaneous and continuing activity of a whole people with a common heritage, acting within a commonality of experience."[3] Whatever their motivating beliefs were at the time, it would be hard to think of a more organic sense of purpose than one in which the citizens not only created their own environments, but did so with what they could produce from the materials on site and all shaped by their own hands.

The spirit of architecture, more than any other human pursuit, including politics, religion, and economics is one that addresses the relatedness between the land, the built environment and human need, including the sculpting of space in ways that nurture our individual and collective spirit.

Everything we build should be as inspiring to its intended purpose as a cathedral is to worship. Architecture at its finest is our human equivalent to the inseparable ways and means of nature. It is the three-dimensional music of life. That architecture which is most beautiful is also, for the long term, the most practical. And when thinking long term, there is no higher calling of architecture than to shape and give life to the physical and spiritual settings we all share.

Environmental Art

Because the places, spaces and systems of community are both functional and everywhere present, it may seem difficult to think of what all this adds up to becoming as being a work of art. It may also be why we spend a great deal of time and money in order to travel thousands of miles to visit special places for brief periods of time, only to return with hundreds of pictures to share with our friends who live in places where we may have resided for years without ever feeling the desire to photograph.

At its best, the art of community provides settings from which we derive strength and identity from the atmosphere of its places and spaces. It is a partnering with the regenerative systems of nature, where beauty and function are one and where everything is related and nothing is ever "thrown out." Anything less than our ability to emulate nature's methods produces all manner of human conflict and suffering. The opposite of waging war, rather than some poetic notion of peace, is all about our ability to create and nurture a spirit of community.

This most demanding of all the arts is so complex that despite the array of speeches and ceremonies dedicated on its behalf, it may be difficult, if not impossible, to find anyone who believes that there will ever be a world without the threat of violence and war. There are endless reasons as to why things have to be as they are. They also coexist with the flicker of hope that there is a better way. The witty Winston Churchill once remarked that we Americans can always be counted on to do absolutely the right thing, just as soon as we've tried and exhausted every other option. Perhaps that thought could be applied to all of humanity. In terms of first trying every other option, could we come to the realization that each and every war, sets the stage for the next and that every new technology designed for defense, can also add to the arsenals and strategies for attack?

Isn't it time for the religions that preach the impossibility of peace on earth to realize that this can play out as a kind of self-fulfilling prophesy? And for those who place their faith in technology, when in history has technology been anything but an amplifier of human behavior for good or ill? The future may not be so much threatened by what we easily call ignorance as it is by the so-called intelligence that in so many ways has a vested interest in conflict.

And finally, isn't it time to expand on our definition of art? Might we want to reconsider well-meaning programs like "two percent for art"? What about the other 98 percent? Haven't we learned from the failures of Chicago's Cabrini Green or Pruitt Igoe in St. Louis. The latter was designed by Minoru Yamasaki, the famed architect for the original World Trade Center. Just 17 years after its celebrated opening, the massive Pruitt-Igoe project had to be entirely demolished. Yamasaki observed that it had deteriorated into a crime-infested disaster, at least in part because he had designed a housing project rather than the far greater complexity of designing for community. We have much to learn not only about the connection between artless development and unwanted behavior, but also what it takes to provide artful environments. Bernard Rudofsky, who was responsible for the MoMA exhibition, put it most clearly, "A town that aspires to being a work of art must be as finite as a painting, or book, or a piece of music." [4]

Everything we've learned and now pursue under the banner of being *smart, green and sustainable* is but the most primitive kind of awakenings compared to the interrelated, cause and effect workings of nature. Unlike nature, we have no long-term single system of accounting. We routinely sell off whatever "pieces" will bring the best price in the short term, rather than worrying about the loss and damage inflicted on the greater system of which the pieces are its component parts. As a result, that which is necessary for life itself becomes nothing but a collection of commodities to be bought and sold.

The Subtleties of Community

The transition from conflict to community is humanity's single-most urgent, complex and integrated quest. Unlike the kind of clarity we associate with opposites like *heaven and hell*, or *war and peace*, the words *conflict and community* describe interdependent differences in which the journey goes beyond any kind of either/or clarity.

The subtleties of this journey are more like the transitional differences from noise to music, from words to meaning, and from structure to architecture. It is a pitched battle, because noise is far easier to produce than music, words are cheap and ever present, while meaning in architecture is hard to come by. With respect to design, even the most dazzling structures can be thoughtlessly cobbled together in ways that may end up being more curious than beautiful. The art of architecture can only be loved into reality. The pursuit of community is all about the journey from commodification to stewardship. Commodification is fragmented, artless and easy. Stewardship is interconnected, artful and challenging.

Just as it is easier to fall down than to get up, as well as it being easier to catch another person's germs than it is to catch their good health, it is far easier to exploit conflict than to nurture community. It is easier to argue than to communicate, and it is far easier to establish the price of anything that can be bought and sold than it is to create and define its value. Price, it seems, needs no defense. Value requires a higher level of understanding than anything more easily shared in the marketplace. Those who trade in the buying and selling of real estate are very careful to separate price from value.

I once received an unforgettable call from an individual who held an interim position where he was responsible for administering a seven-decades-old Foundation that had never been heavily endowed but had created and accumulated a vast collection of priceless treasures. The caller seemed to indicate that he had just discovered an overlooked commodity that needed to be put to work. Here is how he explained this new-found opportunity. "I know it seems unbelievable, but we have no idea what the

Foundation's assets are worth. Can you suggest someone who could assist us in determining the value of what we own?" I was absolutely stunned by the implication of the question. By "value", I worried that what the caller really meant was "price," which could only be realized by selling off and devitalizing the purpose and power of the original collection with respect to why, where and how it had been created. Regrettably, this is exactly what happened.

Unprecedented Urgencies

Properly understood, three observations make designing for community a matter of great urgency. They are not the same, but they are all related. As mentioned in the introduction, the first is occasioned by the geometrically increasing number of people who are all sharing the resources of our single planetary home. The second is our dramatically increasing consumption per capita. And the third is the diversity of human needs, interests and dissimilar demands, all now in ever-closer proximity.

This third observation has always been true for the local habitations of earth. What is unprecedented is that the diversity of human needs and desires, rather than being separated by distance, as has been the case for all of human history, is now both physically and digitally occupying the same space and time with few if any shared rules or agreements concerning our respective beliefs and behaviors.

Having no magic wand other than our instincts for survival and the regenerative lessons of nature, there is a growing urgency for a more integrated view of what we so easily divide into specialties like economics, science, art, and religion. While there is no way to avoid dealing with society's tendency to think of these in their own special terms, we are more and more being influenced by the oneness of the universe. Buckminster Fuller advocated the need for a new kind of designer, one who would be a "synthesis of artist, inventor, mechanic, objective economist and evolutionary strategist."

Italian Hill Towns: Rudofsky wrote about what he called the anachronistic communities like Anticoli Coronado, in the Sabine Mountains near Rome, shown above. According to Rudofsky, "The very thought that modern man could live in communities like these would seem absurd were it not that they are increasingly becoming refuges for city dwellers. People who have not yet been reduced to appendages to automobiles find them a fountain of youth." His observations are epitomized by Positano on the following page, which 500 years ago was a simple fishing village.

Timeless Design: While we easily extol the sustainable pursuits of modern architecture it would be hard for contemporary society to come anywhere near the achievements of Apricale on the Italian Riviera (above) or Val di FaFora or Alberobella, shown on the following page, which have existed for centuries.

ECONOMICS, SCIENCE, ART, AND RELIGION

"When we try to pick anything out by itself, we find

it hitched to everything else in the Universe."

–John Muir

W hat John Muir, the great American environmentalist, observed about the Universe is the ultimate goal of humankind with respect to the earth home we all share. Just as our sun shines no less brightly even though it is related to something greater than itself, the same is true for each of us as citizens of the greater world. What we call "the news" is our 24/7 reminder that we've got a long way to go before seeing ourselves in these terms. Unlike nature, which has no separate departments for economics, science, art and religion, we humans more readily compartmentalize everything into its own special category, too often at the expense of the whole.

The Dismal Science

Financial instruments have been designed for the few without any considerations for the long-term consequence for the many. This was summarized by Philippe Meyer, a former Wall Street trader. "If running the economy off the cliff makes you money, you will do it, and you will do it every day." How this sentiment played out was later observed in

Fortune magazine, "It's been five years since the smartest guys in the room blew up the economy. Bankers betting against the stuff they were selling people. Bankers dispossessing people of homes purchased with loans they had made to the homeowners. Bankers trying to get over on the system in 100 different ways." [1]

The more general manipulative power of economics is outlined by Stephen Marglin, a Harvard Economist and author of *The Dismal Science: How Thinking Like an Economist Undermines Community*. "Over the past four hundred years, the ideology of economics has fostered both the self-interested individual and the market system, and has undermined, and continues to undermine the community."[2] Everything to do with designing, building, living and governing in a market-driven economy has a narrowing effect on the kind of exploration the art of community might otherwise prompt and deserve. It is neither too harsh nor inaccurate to say that much of where we live, learn, work, shop and play has been shaped more by market forces than any other more performance-centered considerations. In the words of one, prominent developer, "Everything associated with where, how, what, and when we build, all comes down to velocity and margin," in other words how fast can whatever it is be rented or sold and at what percent of profit.

A more thoughtful, and I'm pleased to say, a far more successful developer, said essentially the same thing but with far greater commitment to the outcome. Upon reviewing a carefully orchestrated set of plans for a large-scale development, he responded saying, "Considering that this deserves a good deal of thought, it will need to be studied with respect for the art of the possible."

A related insight comes from Charles Handy, a scholar educated at Oxford and MIT. Handy was an executive at the Shell Oil Company, a professor at the London Business School, and one of Britain's most highly acclaimed authors of business books. Writing under the heading, "Clouds on the Horizon," Handy suggests that Adam Smith, the high priest of market economics and of modern capitalism, may well be the most quoted and least read of all authors." Who, Handy asks, knows that Smith wrote this?"

"A profitable speculation is presented as a public good because growth will stimulate demand, and everywhere diffuse comfort and improvement. No patriot or man of feeling could therefore oppose it. But the nature of this growth, in opposition, for example, to older ideas such as cultivation, is that it is at once undirected and infinitely self-generating in the endless demand for all the useless things in the world." [3]

Under the heading, "There is Better News," Handy writing in B*eyond Certainty: The Changing Worlds of Organizations* (1996), adds, "It is now clear that economic growth for all forever is not in the cards. Even if it were, it would be no guarantee of happiness. In the last 20 years the British economy grew by 40%, the German by 50% and the Japanese by 60%, but it is by no means obvious that the Germans and the Japanese are happier. In fact, surveys show the reverse, with the Japanese envious of the lifestyles of almost everyone. Perhaps we will soon cease to pursue the chimera of everlasting economic growth and hearken to Adam Smith's reminder of cultivation as a primary goal." [4] Nothing could accelerate and nurture the pursuit of community more. In its highest sense, this pursuit begins where the singular focus on monetary transactions leaves off. An all-out commitment to creating sustainable communities would favor cultivation over commodification. And in terms of the marketplace a more genuine, long-term sense of values would trump all things short-term, clever and shrewd.

What makes humanity's adventure, from conflict to community, both puzzling and difficult is that on a behavioral level it is occurring in two simultaneous but very different worlds, one very large and the other very small. In terms of science, these two worlds are represented by the differences between quantum theory and relativity. The two worlds of community consist of the local to global battles we wage against each other and the internal battles

that rage within ourselves.
Science and the Arts

When the world of design uses scientific terms like *biophilia*, it reflects an awakening to what Frank Lloyd Wright throughout his entire lifetime called *organic*. We are only now beginning to apply that to the architecture of human settlements. This will demand the best we each have to offer. The art of community is simply unachievable without shared insights, strategies and unending commitment. Individual accomplishments are easy to observe and measure. No such clarity exists for the shared pursuit of community. Nor is it something that can be achieved by an all-out pursuit of the few.

What then, is this seemingly nebulous journey, and if it is all that confusing, what is it that deserves our attention? What do we really mean and feel about the word *community*? Developers use it to describe something for sale, as in golf course or retirement communities. Planners and architects portray communities with colored plans and perspective renderings to, "show how everything will look when finished." We also use the word to describe special groups as in "a community of scholars." Max de Pree, the author of *Leadership is an Art*, says that for leaders, "community" is a magical word.

At its most profound, great art of all kinds is its own measure. It didn't get to be great by way of the auction house, or by the exclusionary power of a patent, or by way of politics, legislation or litigation. Great art, including the art of community, like all other aspects of being human, takes place within the fragmentation of our laws and conventions, but like the life force itself, that which is artful is more timeless.

The success of science is to address both old and new solutions or insights for which the proof is that the findings are replicable. Success in the arts can be considered anything from favorable reviews by one's peers, to that recognized by scholars or the allegiance of a far wider audience.

With respect to the art of architecture, if it isn't worthy of being called art, it isn't worthy of being called architecture. While Frank Lloyd Wright regarded architecture to be the mother art, I have no interest in debating this point, nor does it make any sense to compare the relative rankings of poetry, music, theater, dance or any other artforms, except for one. The highest calling of the art of architecture is far more than anything that can be produced by the architect alone. It is the art in which the brush strokes of the painter, the orchestration of the composer, and the dance directions of choreographer, are all brought together in the artful relationships of life we all share. This artform is nothing less than the cultural relationships between the various interests and contributions of individuals living in balance, both with each other and all together with the life- enriching beauty of nature.

Rather than seeing this as some naïve, unreachable notion of utopia, it is more realistically one of choosing the difficulty and gains of community over the slide into the conflicts that can so easily become our shared paths of least resistance. When conflict is the norm, every other kind of advancement which we may celebrate, only adds to that which threatens our very existence.

We have already mastered the art of painting, music, sculpture and dance. Architecture is celebrated in the design of the world's galleries and concert halls which we visit to be uplifted by the specialties of what we call culture. Sooner or later we will want to understand that the artform we need most consists of the brushstrokes, choreography and orchestration of community. That to which we've given "two percent" and treated as the specialty of "public art," must give way to a far deeper understanding and recognition of our human purpose. If this weren't so essential, we would likely regard it to be impossible. The greater truth is that we have no other acceptable choice.

Unlike the scientist's search for a universal proof, the worthiness of art is more like what the poet Walt Whitman had to say about wisdom. "Wisdom cannot be taught in schools, it cannot be passed from one having it to another who does not. Wisdom is not susceptible of proof. It is its own proof."[5] Many would say this is also true of that which makes possible the pretense and practice of religion. "Pretense" is not used here in a pejorative sense, but only to acknowledge that there are many differing practices of religion, each claiming to represent the one true way.

The Power and Complexity of Religion

Huston Smith is a remarkable man who spent more than half a century exploring the world's deepest beliefs, not as competing theologies, but to get at what he refers to as the "water table" of their similar missions. The tenacity of his study was extraordinary, including the degree to which he immersed himself in the study of Hinduism, Buddhism, Confucianism, Christianity, Judaism and Islam. His summary conclusion was that he saw nothing but good in each, which he expressed by way of two overriding conclusions.

The first is that all great religions, at their core, are cultivators of the uniquely human virtues of "intelligence, compassion, creativity, beauty and goodness." The second is that those who devote their lives to such studies have yet to find any record of a civilization that didn't have a religious component so thoroughly woven into the social fabric of the time that it is impossible to isolate it as an independent element.

If he stopped here his views might be embraced by all religious leaders, but he goes further, observing that "Jesus is called the Prince of Peace. He taught that we should even love our enemies." To this Smith adds, "I could put on my religious historian's cap and go through all the major religions, showing that 'the founders of each, all taught the very same ideas in their own idiom." [6]

Quite unlike what Houston Smith observed, others have described this coming together of more than one fundamentalist belief as having only three possible outcomes; *convert, accommodate, or kill.* In the history of humanity many have been converted, and millions have been killed.

Harvey Cox was a Professor of Divinity at Harvard where he taught for 34 years. He is widely considered to be one of the most influential authors regarding protestant theology. His 1965 best-selling book *The Secular City* is devoted to linking the "coming of age" of religion where individual and shared beliefs come together with the designed settings for community. In his words, "two hallmarks of our era are the rise of civilization and the collapse of traditional religion." [7]

Adding to the battles we humans wage against each other in the name of religion, are the battles we are jointly waging against the earth we all share. Lloyd Gerring, a professor and religious studies scholar is among a growing chorus of spiritual leaders who are sounding the alarm. "For centuries the Western world has encouraged us to believe that our future is in the hands of a benevolent and all-powerful God and that we have been placed here on earth to prepare for an eternal destiny elsewhere. Consequently we have focused our attention to the heavenly realm and devalued the natural physical world." [8]

Among humanity's greatest challenges is to get beyond our record of exploitation, death and destruction in order to redirect that energy and its corresponding trillions of dollars to the benefit of life, creativity and community. Failure to achieve this level of cooperation will leave the world in a never-ending escalation of destruction that no amount of military strength can hope to resolve.

While explorations concerning religion have dominated scholarly interest all throughout history, consider just how fragile and judgmental our own beliefs remain. Robert Wright, is a brilliant author and former teacher of philosophy at Princeton and religion at the University of Pennsylvania. Here is how he expresses the shared experiences of millions.

"Back around age nine, at the Immanuel Baptist Church in El Paso, Texas, I had felt the call of God and walked to the front of the church as a visiting evangelist issued the 'invitation' – the call for unredeemed sinners to accept Jesus as their savior. A few weeks later I was baptized by the church's minister...three decades later, another Baptist minister was placing me in the general vicinity of Satan." [9]

This occurred as Robert Wright was being denounced from the pulpit of his mother's church. It is unlikely that either fundamentalist Muslims, or fundamentalist Christians would find much to like in what he had to say in response.

"...Who is right? Is Islam a religion of peace? Of war? In one sense, the answer is the same as it would be for any other Abrahamic religion. Religions, as should be clear by now, have their good moments and their bad moments, their good scriptures and their bad scriptures. The ratio of good to bad scriptures varies among the Abrahamic faiths, but in all religions it is possible for benign interpretation of scripture to flourish." [10]

What should interest us most is that Robert Wright, explores and reveals the forces that have repeatedly moved the Abrahamic faiths away from belligerence and intolerance to a higher moral plane. He shows how these forces could let these faiths reassert their deep proclivity toward harmony and reconciliation. What's more, his analysis raises the prospect of a second kind of reconciliation: the reconciliation of science and religion. All this is to say that we can choose the cost, difficulty, and the savagery of our mutual loss, or the cost and difficulty of living in community.

Searching for the Unity of Life

John Robbins, recipient of the Rachel Carson Award and the Albert Schweitzer Humanitarian Award, writes about the African Pygmies, who are among the world's cultures that have endured the longest and have placed the highest value on human relationships. "There is no crime, there are no police, and no one is ever punished...Their language has no word for hatred and no word for war." Robbins quotes the late Jean-Pierre Hallet, an internationally renowned ethnologist, concluding that the whole substance and meaning of the Pygmy religion is "Be good to other people. Respect, protect and preserve." [11] Justice Oliver Wendell Holmes echoed this when he said simply, "My religion is based on the first two words of the Lord's prayer."

Having studied the amazing records of societies unlike our own, here is how Robbins sees the important variables facing us for the future. "The choices that we make today, as to how we treat each other, the way we raise our children, and the kinds of families and communities we create, will determine how the future unfolds. If we treat each other another way, if we encourage and uphold our essential goodness and capacity for loving connections, we can nurture a society of people who are healthy and whole and whose lives will bring healing and joy to those they touch." [12]

In spite of the thousands of sectarian beliefs that divide us, might we consider adopting something like the beliefs that have stood the test of time for centuries as our way-of-life religion for a world that works? Because there are countless smart people who don't think this is possible, perhaps all that means is that a workable future will depend on expanding or redefining what we mean by "being smart".

Religion is very much like technology. We generally have little reason to talk about either unless the discussion centers on their awesome power. But at that level, not only can they dominate the news, they can influence the future of humanity. Just as technology can extend our human ability to create or destroy by how we use what we invent, religion affords the same choices by how we act on what we believe.

What a different world it would be if we could all be not only satisfied but inspired by this observation from John Steinbeck. "...It is a strange thing that most of the feeling we call religious, most of the mystical outcrying which is one of the most prized and used and desired reactions for our species, is really the understanding and the attempt to say that man is related to the whole thing, related inextricably to all reality, known and unknowable...that all things are one thing and that one thing is all things..." [13]

The unity of nature has been divided by those who look for answers by way of an unending scientific exploration as opposed to those for whom the answers have long since been revealed by the scriptures. Both are irrefutable, science by way of replicable testing, allowing for new insights to be a normal part of the quest, and religion because there was a time and place when all truths and prophecies were revealed for all time. The power of art including the work of Michelangelo and Bach is that it allows us to dream, think and act outside the more defined boundaries of both the methods of science and the dictates of beliefs.

Beyond the War of Words

If there is any one sensation that so easily bypasses our learned likes and dislikes, as well as all that we hate, love, fear, believe in or don't understand, it is most likely to be associated with tears. Crying is that wordless sensation that occurs at the deepest level of what makes us who we are. And as we all know, the feelings that accompany tears occur when we are more removed from the more obvious kinds of measures. It is this unspeakable treasure of our humanness that underlies whatever it is that favors the sharing of life, love and everything that is most genuine and lasting.

Religion at its non-denominational core can be a short cut to "knowing" in that it can provide the clarity of faith in the unseen, triggered, by our own response to beauty, both natural and man-made. Religion at its worst, can be a force for dividing us in ways that need no armies. The battle is one we carry within our own hearts, minds, and prejudices.

In what may seem as heretical to some, Steven Hawking and others have referred to the science of physics as a search to know the **mind** of God. Frank Lloyd Wright always put a capital "N" on nature, saying it is the **body** of God. To fundamentalists, the Bible is the inerrant **word** of God. And history is replete with battles in which all sides have set out to destroy the other in the **name** of God.

Given the many seemingly insoluble issues that divide us, might we agree, that the nature of earth, and the universe of which it is a part, along with the multiverses, and everything to do with life itself, are the only realities that aren't matters of our own human invention? It may seem impossible to envision that the day may come when the adherents to our many and varied doctrines might find their way to a shared set of practices and beliefs, yet here we all are, sharing, the beauty of earth that unites and makes possible our very existence.

If we can't find any other agreement within the terms of our own invented beliefs, how about taking a closer look at what most, if not all religions, attribute to the creation of God. The more we probe into space, the more physicists are telling us that we live on a perfect planet, the only known planet with liquid water. One with a perfect level of gravitational pull, with perfect soil for growing crops, perfect rivers and streams with abundant fish, a perfect atmosphere for protection from radiation and a perfect range of minerals to harvest as ingredients to supply our every need.

Thus, starting from where we are today, might we, for the sanctity of all we've been given, come to realize that our growing awareness of the creation may be the only evidence of the divine that we can all share?

Shortly before his death, I had the privilege of hearing the Rev. William Sloane Coffin give one of his last addresses. It occurred at the Chautauqua Institution in western New York. Having suffered from a stroke, he had to be helped to the podium where he turned his condition to a most endearing opening. Noting that the stroke had impaired his speech, he made reference to George Bernard Shaw saying, "Richard Wagner's music is not as bad as it sounds." Coffin followed this with, "I hope my message is better than it sounds." He then took careful aim at all of us." If we are to be equal to the times we live in and to the greater problems the future will bring, we had better learn to scorn trifles and strive to be far more imaginative and more generous in spirit. Above all, I believe we need to claim the kinship of all people, to recover the prophetic insight that we belong one to another, every one of us from the Pope to the lowliest wino on the planet. From a religious perspective, that's the way God made us. From a Christian perspective, Christ died to keep us that way, which means that our sin is only and always "that we put asunder what God has joined together."

"Make love your aim, not biblical inerrancy, nor purity, nor obedience to holiness codes. Make love your aim, for though I speak with the tongues...of angels – musicians, poets, preachers, you are being addressed; and though I understand all mysteries and have all knowledge – professors, your turn; and though I give all my goods to feed the poor – radicals take note; and though I give my body to be burned – the very stuff of heroism; but have not love, it profiteth me nothing. I doubt if in any other scriptures of the world there is a more radical statement of ethics: if we fail in love, we fail in all things else."

Coffin then went on to suggest that we might all guard against being too certain and content with our beliefs. "There is no smaller package in the world than that of a person all wrapped up in himself. Love is our business; if we can't love, we're out of business. And all this Christians learn primarily through the words and deeds inspired by love divine – all loves excelling, joy of heaven to earth come down."

The complexities of modern life are testing all certainties. According to Robert Wright, this is the way it's supposed to be. "Life on earth was, from the beginning, a machine for generating meaning and then deepening it, a machine that created the potential for good and began to fulfill it. And, though the machine also created the potential for bad – and did plenty of fulfilling on that front – it now finally shows signs of raising the ratio of good to bad; or, at the very least, of giving the human species that option, along with powerful incentives to exercise it." [14]

The Power of Faith

Everything about life from birth to death and beyond involves faith. In its highest sense, faith is transcendent. In the words of Manly Palmer Hall, faith " has inspired the arts, enriched literature and poetry, and added luster to the learned professions. No one is better for being a materialist. No one is stronger because of unbelief. The work of the world, the progress in all departments of our social order, is the result of practical idealism. Great individuals always believe in something greater than themselves. By this belief they are inspired to overcome those obstacles which are always cast in the way of greatness."[15]

The world of design that we need most is one firmly rooted in a positive faith in the future. Lloyd Geering suggests that we are moving in that direction. "The wind of the Spirit is blowing. One indication is the up-heaval that is shaking and renewing Christianity. Faith, rather than beliefs, is once again becoming its defining quality, and this reclaims what faith meant during its earliest years...All the signs suggest we are poised to enter a new Age of the Spirit and that the future will be a future of faith." [16]

FROM PLATO TO THE PRESENT

"If you go back into the history of humankind, you find that in all great
cultures – the Greek, the Babylonian, the Chinese, the Japanese, and our
own – everything begins with a dream."

–Laurens van der Post

One of the most extraordinary ideas that accompanied the
founding of the United States was the sovereignty of the
individual, unlike the core of all Utopian socialism which is the
sovereignty of the plan. Plato provides a good account of the latter. His
ideal community was to be limited in size and well placed with respect to
the natural environment. Above all else were the carefully considered and
enforced rules of behaviors that would be necessary to achieve and sustain
what he had in mind. If we find things to admire about the ancient Greeks,
Plato's thoughts about the ideal community should not be among those we
are ready to pursue.

Both Plato's Republic, and Sir Thomas More's Utopia, were most likely
prompted by their states of social disintegration, including the hopeless
disorder of their respective times and circumstances. For Plato this was
occasioned by the aftermath of the Peloponnesian War. For Thomas More, his
pursuit of the ideal community was part of his vision for bridging between the
Middle Ages and the awakening interests and promise of the Renaissance.

Plato wanted to overcome what he saw of the indolence, meanness and
vicissitudes of the populous. He established an arbitrary maximum of
5,040 people for each community and spoke eloquently about "a place for

every man and every man in his place." This was all to be assured by the Guardians, the chosen few who were granted an extraordinary power to administer "medical lies." As part of this amazing "right," they would decide, declare and limit the status and ability of each newborn.

Not to be overlooked in Plato's pursuit of a community "without servitude, avarice, compulsion and indolence," were two special provisions, which among other things did away with the pettiness of law. The first provision was that children who were, for whatever reason, judged to be unfit, were considered as "weeds" to be eliminated accordingly. In the second, Plato forbad any laws that would get in the way of graft, bribery and theft. Altogether this would not seem to leave much for 21st century democracy to explore and emulate.

For a concise summary of the shortcomings of both Plato and 2000 years later, Thomas More's Utopia, this is what Kamal Amin, a fellow architect and author had to say in his 2009 book, *Excursions*:

> "Plato associated aristocracy with communal living. He stated that the chief cause of discord was rooted in private property. He reserved a privileged and refined form of communal living for the rulers, guardians, philosophers and scientists. The lower classes, he decided, could own private property, quarrel among themselves, breed promiscuously and deteriorate physically and mentally...In 1517, Sir Thomas More, published his book *'Utopia'*. He invents a society where all goods are provided by collective labor, and it is up to the head of each family to partake of these goods seeking what the family needs. Then Sir Thomas writes in the chapter titled *On their lives together*, 'There is more than enough of everything and there is no fear that anyone will ask for more than he needs. For why would he be likely to seek too much, when he knows for certain that his needs will always be met? A man is made greedy and grasping ether by the fear of need (a fear common to all creatures)...This kind of vice has no place at all in the life of the Utopians".

Amin sums this up saying, "So, Sir Thomas did not only invent an ideal society, but in order to make it work, he also invented an ideal creature to inhabit that society who is immune to human frailties." [1]

Four and a half centuries later, another brilliant friend, Buckminster Fuller, made the same mistake. In his 1969, *Utopia or Oblivion, the Prospects for Humanity*, Fuller first outlines all the reasons to be optimistic concerning the unprecedented success of the future. Rather than relying on the manipulation of the citizens to create a more perfect community, Fuller is painstakingly clear about the beneficial, wealth-creating evolution of technology – far too much so in my opinion. For like Thomas More, he comes to the conclusion that requires leaving out the vagaries and tendencies of human behavior. In keeping with Fuller's thesis, as soon as humanity realized that there were sufficiently abundant resources to take care of everyone, there would be no reason to steal or hoard. Viewed from the present, it seems there is an obvious flaw in this reasoning. That which is made possible by technology alone, proceeds at a very different pace than the comparative snails pace of change with respect to human behavior. This is especially true for those characteristics that are always seeking to take advantage of whatever the circumstances may be. Having enough to go around, always seems to translate into some version of that means even more for the few.

A very human dynamic that separates the present from the past is the degree to which society was once more cohesive by way of clans, tribes and families. Present societal relationships have become far more separated not only in terms of culture but by way of age, technology, conveniences and interests. It could be said that the new family has gone beyond biology and necessity to an unprecedented condition in which "families" are created either by circumstance or choice.

The Primary Goal of Civilization

Unlike the clarity made possible in the proposals from both Plato and Thomas More, the present is a difficult but positive time of adjustments between the young and the old and between the "haves" and the "have-nots." On the positive side of the "haves" are those who are investing billions of dollars in support of the health, education and well-being of those who need it most. Millions of others, including many of the "have-nots," are creating a new economy by way of the kind of sharing that replaces or augments ownership.

Common to both the so-called rich and poor is that they are, each in their own ways, addressing the need for community, which is quite different from sharing the wealth by fear. Wil and Ariel Durrant's eleven volume, *The Story of Civilization*, totals just under **10,000** pages. In the briefest possible terms, their socioeconomic conclusion, freely translated is that, throughout history just about the time that poor people were planning to kill off the rich, the rich people found a way to give them something.

At some level we might all agree that given the riches of the 21st century, no one should go without food, health care, housing or any other of the basic provisions for life. What we've not yet figured out is how to address the unintended consequences as to how these "rights" can be delivered without causing unintended injury.

Bob Schwartz was a partner with Margaret Mead and operator of the famed Tarrytown Institute. In a reflective moment, he once shared with me what he called the sad reality for liberals like himself. Quoting him directly, "Every time government finds a way to create a new entitlement to benefit those who seem to need it the most, it results in a weakening of the recipients resolve and commitment toward self-sufficiency."

During the time that I was writing this chapter, a most unexpected voice connected Plato to the present in a single sentence. On April 9, 2013, Supreme Court Justice Clarence Thomas was interviewed on C-SPAN by Ken Gromley and Thomas Hardiman regarding his life and career. The Justice spoke of cultural values, including the importance of respecting and preserving beautiful architecture. At one point in the interview he urged that we invest more time in reading, "more time on Aristotle or Socrates, more time reading Frank Lloyd Wright."

UTOPIA OR OBLIVION

"If we don't do the impossible, we shall be faced with the unthinkable."

–Petra Kelly

I n addition to the gift of working with Frank Lloyd Wright, it afforded those of us who shared his life an opportunity to learn from the distinguished individuals who would come for a time to be part of the Taliesin Community. These guests ranged from artists and statesmen, to scientists, hollywood actors, and captains of industry.

My favorite of all the guests and the one I spent the most time with was R. Buckminster Fuller, or Bucky as he was called by his friends. Few, if any individuals or groups have ever sought to combine creative imagination with engineering science, informing both with data that others had either never measured nor analyzed as components of an overall and coordinated system. For Bucky, his comprehensive way of seeing was as normal as breathing in and breathing out. Recounting how it all came about, Fuller offers this as though it were normal for everyone.

"Most children like to collect things. At four, I started to collect documents of my own development as correlated with world patterns of developing technology. Beginning in 1917, I determined to employ my already rich case history, as objectively as possible, in documenting the life of a suburban New Englander, born in the Gay Nineties (1895) – the year automobiles were introduced, the wireless telegraph and the automatic screw machine were invented and X-rays were discovered; having his boyhood in the turn of the century; and maturing during humanity's epochal graduation from the inert, materialistic 19th into the dynamic, abstract 20th century. I named my documentation, The Chronofile..." The young Bucky then jumps to concluding that Sir Isaac Newton's normally 'at rest' world was about to be turned on its head by what he called "Einstein's normally dynamic, omni-integrating world culture to which change has come to seem evolutionarily inevitable." [1]

In 1917 at age 22 Fuller concluded that he would see more change in his lifetime then had occurred between his "father's, grandfather's, great-grandfather's, and great-great-great-grandfather's successive generations," all of whom attended Harvard. Continuing with his big picture way of seeing, he noted that the average lifespan expectancy since the year he was born had increased from 42 to 70 years of age. While the extent of his travel was exceptional, he nonetheless proposed that in the year of his birth (1895) the average total distance individuals traveled was 30,000 miles. By 72 he had logged more than 3,000,000 miles and in addition to a great deal of local travel he was now circling the globe several times each year. To underscore what he was trying to say about humanity's geometrically increasing technological advantage, he discounted the 3,000,000 miles he traveled during his first 72 years by pointing out that the Gemini astronauts exceeded that distance in a week. [2]

Like many people who see the future in terms of the geometrically increasing range of technology, if Bucky had a weakness, it would be his somewhat oversimplified view of the vagaries and interests of human behavior. For example, one of his beliefs was that if governmental restrictions would get out of the way, one new idea could feed the world.

To illustrate what he meant by freedom from the constraints of government, he maintained that all good ideas were created in what he called "the outlaw area," meaning for example, at sea beyond the limits of governmental laws, codes or ordinances, or in space, or in the military. Unlike Bucky's earlier pronouncement, many "one new ideas" have been made that have done more to enrich their patent holders than to feed the world. He shared his awareness of this when he said that without the patents he held on his work, no one would have ever heard of him, as others would have simply taken his work as their own. Nonetheless, his buoyant faith in what he called "humanity's regenerative spirit" remains, most inspiring.

Our Very Human Challenges

The year was 1927, when Bucky, whose life work is now considered to be a global resource, found himself walking alone along Chicago's Lake Michigan, feeling so useless and so much of a burden on his family that he was considering suicide. I recount this not simply to add a biographical note but to illustrate how closely related our human instincts can be between life-threatening despair and unbounded enthusiasm for all that is yet to be. And that which we experience as individuals, is part of what accompanies the challenging pursuits of our shared world experiences.

The Buckminster Fuller so revered today always lamented that there were so few people capable of understanding the unprecedented success that he wrote and spoke about, saying that the only things standing in our way were our own doubts, fears, and ignorance. But consider this evidence that he was not immune to the human challenges that affect us all. The Bucky most of the world knows, either by personal contact or by way of his inventions, writings and lectures – to his dying day was a paragon of faith, hope and inspiration. Yet in 1927, a series of financial reversals made the unemployed Fuller feel not only like a failure but such a burden that he felt that the proceeds from his life insurance would be more beneficial to his family than a continuation of his presence.

He walked along the lake going over and over hours of internal debate, centering on "life or death." This continued until at one point he heard a voice: "From now on you never need await temporal attestation to your thoughts. You think the truth. You are fulfilling your role if you apply yourself to converting your experiences to the highest advantage of others." [3]

After his near-death experience, Fuller began to cast aside what he considered to be the limitations of traditional thinking. He began studying and published what became known as *The World Resources Inventory*. This amazing book showed how the proper use of resources would revolutionize our traditional thinking about employment. That the whole idea of working just to live would become obsolete, that ownership would be replaced by a far more efficient society of shared use. He calculated, and later proved that our U.S. energy system was five percent efficient, with 95 percent being wasted.

In the 1950's, he announced that humanity's problems were not political and as such, politicians would be of little use in the radically new environment he saw coming, much of which is today's reality. If he were able to help society move beyond the seemingly stillborn nature of its political initiatives, he would feel that his prophecy had been fulfilled.

Bucky was way ahead of his time in suggesting that ownership was illogical in what he saw would be an emerging new society. He envisioned a new kind of abundance that would evolve from an ownership and product–oriented society to a service-oriented system. This was long before the shared use of everything from cars, planes, boats, housing, clothing, jewelry and much more, had become not only commonplace but also a growth industry.

His feelings in this direction were shaped by his own lifestyle. Traveling around the world at an average of once every year, his entire experience and use of "resources" were all shared.

By way of his around-the-world teaching of *The World Game*, he proposed that there would come a time when the world's people would be able to operate with the confidence of adequate resources to support everyone on Earth. He went further to say that when this happened, payment for the use of these resources would become obsolete.

Fuller knew that his world game was not only fully dependent on a continual updating of his *World Resources Inventory*, but that his vision was predicated on an unprecedented degree of global cooperation. Because he had no illusions about this happening, he believed that things would have to get worse before they got better. And when that happened, the seeds planted by *The World Game* would be there to flower and enrich us all. Bucky maintained the faith that we would one day achieve an unprecedented level of cooperative success, for no other reason than in pursuit of our own self-interests.

The Little Honey Bee

He enjoyed telling of his time with a group of Russian scientists who were insisting that the cooperative spirit of communism was a better path to discovery and success than the highly competitive nature of capitalism. The Russians saw themselves as working together, sharing information for the benefit of all, quite unlike what they imagined to be the competition involving secrets between one U.S. team and another.

Fuller's disarming response was to suggest that we were all more like the little honey bee who goes in pursuit of sweet nectar and while doing so, inadvertently pollinates the flower with its tail. This response to the Russian scientists who posed an either/or proposition, wanting for their side to be right and our side to be wrong, provided a very valuable insight for understanding the spirit of community.[4]

It is human to harbor our own convictions as to how we treat the cause and effects of our behaviors, and procedures. Unlike the honey bee who required nothing but instinct to achieve success, we humans have been given the blessings and burdens that come with the ability to think for ourselves.

Buckminster Fuller was a liberating resource just by way of his uncommon pursuits. In addition to our conversations at both Taliesin and Taliesin West, I had the privilege of leading others through his World Game workshops, which in the words of the World Game Institute were all about creating, "a global perspective, along with a positive vision of the future and the means for achieving it."

Bucky combined his visionary philosophy with the most specific kinds of surveys and statistical back-up, including his list of 29 human wants from, "abundant supplies of nutrients and culturally appropriate food," to "access to spiritual growth and fulfillment." The word "ownership: is nowhere to be found on his carefully selected list of "wants."

The list released in 1993 was followed by 19 conditions concerning what the "World Does Not Want," ranging from the starvation-related deaths per year and the tons of pollution released into the atmosphere." [5]

Bucky's Children

Stephanie Smith is among the prominent, innovative and effective participants and advocates for the variety of ways that shared use is replacing or augmenting ownership. As a Harvard-trained architect she is also at the forefront of everything to do with mass-produced, sustainable and alternative approaches to the idea of community.

Inspired by the liberating influence of Buckminster Fuller, Smith in her own work and words has taken up a question he posed as one of her central themes; "How can we make the world work for 100 percent of humanity in the shortest possible time through spontaneous cooperation without ecological damage or disadvantage to anyone." [6]

Stewart Brand is another of the important trend-setting, liberating heroes of independent thinking to have been inspired by Bucky. Brand's name is familiar to many as the creator of the *Whole Earth Catalog* which first appeared in July 1968 as a six-page mimeograph before going on to win the National Book Award. Brand's featured selection of tools and ideas were launched with his challenging Do-It-Yourself statement of purpose: "We are as gods and we might as well get good at it."

Brand was a Stanford-trained biologist who became in his words, "in the thrall of Buckminster Fuller...Fuller had put out this idea that there's no use trying to change human nature. It has been the same for a very long time. Instead go after the tools. New tools make new practices. Better tools make better practices." [7]

One of Fuller's easiest to visualize applications of, "don't try to change the human, simply refine the design," is the engineered banking of high-way curves. The drivers simply do what they've always done, while the design of the highway provides for a greater measure of safety.

In one of his Taliesin visits, Fuller said, "I don't see what Frank sees in me. We're so different." Later that weekend, Wright offered an explanation. "Bucky's an engineer who is interested in architecture and I'm an architect who is interested in engineering." I remember thinking at the time that this was a grossly inadequate answer. What they had in common is that in life and work, they symbolized and inspired the world to think and feel beyond any preconceived limitations of the possible. Wright had his way of professing and demonstrating that form and function were one. Bucky's version was to say, "I never design for beauty, but if one of my designs turns out to not be beautiful, I know there is something wrong and I start all over again."

I was looking forward to what was to be a collaboration between Wright and Fuller in the design of a series of movie theaters. The early sketches were circular in plan with one of Fuller's low-rise geodesic domes resting lightly on a Wright-designed, sloping stone base that tied everything together and to the ground.

It would have been great fun to see the evolution of this collaboration, but it was not to be. The client was Mike Todd, the flamboyant creator of the movie, "Around the World in 80 Days." It was shortly after a visit to Taliesin West with his wife, Elizabeth Taylor, that Mike Todd died in a private airplane crash, ending the Wright/Fuller commission.

As for Wright's feeling for Bucky, beyond the words he spoke at Taliesin, this is an except from a review he wrote for Fuller's 1938 publication of *Nine Chains to the Moon.*

"Buckminster Fuller – you are the most sensible man in New York, truly sensitive. Nature gave you antennae, long-range finders you have learned to use. I find almost all your prognosticating nearly right – much of it dead right, and I love you for the way you think. To address you directly will be a hell of a way of reviewing your book – I know. I should write all around you, take you apart, and put you together again to show – between the lines – how much bigger my own mind is than yours and how much smarter than you I can be with it and leave the essence of your thought untouched.

But I couldn't do it if I would and I wouldn't if I could. To say that you have now a good style of your own in saying very important things is only admitting something unexpected. To say you are the most sensible man in New York isn't saying much for you – in that pack of caged fools. And everybody who knows you knows you are extraordinarily sensitive...

Faithfully, your admirer and friend, more power to you – you valuable 'unit'."

Frank Lloyd Wright,
Spring Green, Wisconsin,
August 8th, 1938

In the fall of 1967, I received a letter from Fuller, regarding the 1938 publication of his *Nine Chains to the Moon*. The book included 22 prognostications, which he was eager to establish for the record, knowing that many years later others would likely say, "that is no prognostication, I always knew that was so." The following paragraph from his letter refers to what Wright called him. He also mentions that much of what he predicted three decades earlier had come true.

"Frank's wonderfully friendly and loving review of the prognostication will always be cherished by me. Frank's reference to me as a 'unit' is because, in 1927, I introduced the phrase 'unit' as utility units, kitchen units, etc., into the architectural vernacular as well as introduction of the word 'decked' taken from my Navy experiences. I use 'decked' as in floors, etc. Frank was amused by my term and his use of it in connection with me may now serve to clarify to you what I am saying. The term 'unit' is now familiarly accepted by society making its use seeming ageless. While many of my prognostication did not come true within the ten-year period, many have come in at a later date, and some of them are now about to be fulfilled.

With my personal regard to you and a request that you convey my affectionate esteem to Mrs. Wright.

Faithfully yours,

R. Buckminster Fuller,
November 22, 1967

TECHNOLOGY AND ITS LIMITS

"It is appallingly clear that our technology has surpassed our humanity."

–Albert Einstein

The promise of technology, on its own terms, has and will continue to make possible that which exceeds our wildest imagination. Science fiction, it seems, is having a hard time competing with the discoveries of our growing insights concerning everyday realities. "Today, a street stall in Mumbai can access more information, maps, strategies, academic papers, price trends, future markets, and other data than a U.S. president could only a few decades ago."[1] If this were the only measure of our human successes, each and every scientific breakthrough would bring us ever closer to the many utopian visions that have never seen the light of day.

There are those who believe that humanity is on a kind of automatic pilot in the direction of unimaginable success. Buckminster Fuller, went so far as to suggest that the majority of us are too fear-bound to realize the "success that humanity has hanging over its head." His faith in technology over anything to do with human behavior was made clear when he proclaimed, "If you were to shut down the activities of industry, within six months the world's people would all starve to death. If, on the other hand, all the politicians in the world were put into orbit, no one would know they were gone!"[2]

A clear prophecy of Fuller's faith as advanced into the digital age is set forth in *Abundance: The Future is Better Than You Think*. "Imagine a world of nine billion people with clean water, nutritious food, affordable housing, personalized education, top-tier medical care, and nonpolluting, ubiquitous energy. Building this better world is humanity's greatest challenge."[3] Being inspired by the comprehensive nature of what the authors asked us to imagine, I went immediately to the index, feeling certain that I would be directed to passages focused on the design and behavioral role of *community*. Instead and with respect to Einstein's observation at the beginning of this chapter, I found only a single entry, "Community Computer Center."

The book quotes Stewart Brand whose work was described in the prior chapter. Extending Brand's faith in what could be achieved with the right kind of tools, the authors of *Abundance*, add, "If Moore's law and exponential thinking have taught us anything, it's that what fills a room today will soon require no more than a pocket."[4] The reference here is to Moore's prediction that the processor chips that determine the range of computational power will double in speed every 18 months. This has held true for decades and is likely to hold true for additional decades to come.

A useful and certainly relevant observation would be to acknowledge that there is no "Moore's Law" for predicting the positive doubling of wise and caring behavior. Sooner or later we are going to have to accept both the limitations and threats made possible when our most impressive tools, meet up with the variety of our human intentions. While it was technology that made 9/11 possible, it was human beliefs and behaviors that determined its tragic outcome.

There are two kinds of technologies, both of which may appear worthy, if not miraculous, but they are not the same. The first extends our human abilities and tendencies, including machines required for flight, satellites, wireless and digital transmission. These are all amplifiers of our interests and desires, all of which can be used for good or ill.

The other category of innovation is that which can reduce our consumption and abuse of the non-renewable resources of earth, including fresh water, the mining of minerals, the clear cutting of forests, and the lessening or removal of the poisons we daily put into the soil and release into the atmosphere. Thus the greatest innovations are not only those that increase our human power, but make it more possible to do the right things.

It's doing the right thing that requires more than technological advances alone, as Thom Hartmann describes in *The Last Hours of Ancient Sunlight*. "…recycling won't save the world, birth control won't save the world, and saving what little is left of the rainforests won't save the world. Even if all these good things were fully implemented, our fundamental problem would still remain, and will inevitably be repeated. Even cold fusion and the elimination of the need for oil, with free electricity for everybody, will not save the world. Nothing but changing our way of seeing and understanding the world can produce real, meaningful, and lasting change…and that change in perspective will naturally lead us to begin to control our populations, save our forests, re-create community, and reduce our wasteful consumption."[5]

The human behaviors that lie at the heart of community have their own predictable staying power. Popularly known as the "Seven Deadly Sins," they all started long before, and will most likely outlive, Moore's amazing law.

It took only 63 years from the time of the Wright Brother's 59-second flight at Kitty Hawk to the landing of humans on the moon. More than 2000 years of preaching and teaching based on the examples and words of the prophets have brought us two world wars, with a succession of more localized battles raging somewhere on the planet ever since, with no end in sight.

The geometrically increasing pace of everything digital is making us giddy, no one more so than Google's Eric Schmidt. "From the dawn of civilization until 2003, humankind generated five exabytes of data. Now we produce five exabytes every two days…and the pace is accelerating."[6]

The Difference Between Data and Wisdom

In the most comprehensive sense of its use, computerized power and the data it makes possible is an extraordinary tool, but like all tools, everything depends on how they are used. It takes nothing away from what the digital world makes possible to consider this achievement in terms of its human use beyond the obvious metrics of miniaturization, speed, storage, search, and sharing. This obvious and extraordinary record of what the digital revolution has made possible speaks for itself. But might we at least consider some questions that are more cultural than technological, and far more related to wisdom than data?

• Would, for example, Shakespeare have had a more lasting and greater impact on the world, if only he had access to a computer?

• Would the works of Bach have touched us more deeply if only he could have had a synthesizer?

• Would Rembrandt's insights into color, form, light and dark have been enhanced if he had a spectroscope?

• Will we become a more caring society as soon as we are able to colonize other planets?

• Will the doubling of computational power every 18 months as per Moore's law help us to love one another?

• Will we one day be able to become accomplished musicians without all that tedious practicing and rehearsing?

• Will humans eventually be able to outlive the limits of biology as some are now predicting?

Rather than trying to answer these questions and a host of others that could be asked with sincere intent, they are raised to focus attention on that which is too easily ignored. There is nothing more convincing and certain of itself than anything that can be quantified with a number. Because we like to be certain, we crave numbers like the proverbial bottom line of the nation's gross domestic product, return on investment, the metrics of all athletic events from sand lot baseball to the Olympics, and everything to do with what the dazzling computational power of the digital revolution makes possible.

"For a society to prosper not only technologically but in ways that address the quality of our lives, we must think differently than ever before. Ideas, not technology, founded America and changed the world. What prevents us now from generating the sound, creative and critical thinking so needed today? What so limits the creativity of governments, professional societies, universities and think tanks?"[7]

If ever there was a need for a two worlds understanding that distinguishes the reach and essence of technology from that of our behaviors, that time is now. It takes nothing away from the amazing accomplishments of the timely to reflect on our need for the power and regenerative spirit of the timeless.

Consider the question implied by this oft-repeated comparison: "If we can put a man on the moon and bring him back safely, why can't we achieve the far easier task of simply living together right here on earth? Dr. Mihaly Csikszentmihalyi, a professor and former chairman of the University of Chicago's Department of Psychology offers this answer: "Progress is relatively fast in fields that apply knowledge to the material world, such as physics or genetics. But it is painfully slow when knowledge is to be applied to modify our own habits and desires, in other words, our daily and long term behaviors."[8]

Dr. Csikszentmihalyi's description of the difference between humanity's tools, with the influence of its beliefs and behaviors, lies at the heart of human history. What is not so clear about our human future is how we will address the balance between the kind of tool-like clarity that can be measured in numbers, determined by dollars and demonstrated for all to see, as opposed to the beliefs and behaviors that remain as puzzling as ever.

There is a Sufi saying that "to the hammer, everything is a nail." To the 21st Century technologist, for any given problem there is, or soon will be, a digital breakthrough. The hope and praise accorded "smart cities" centers on the digital ability to reduce greenhouse gas emissions along with providing more efficient control over everything from the production and use of materials and systems, to the conservation of water while providing for the more efficient flow of traffic on land, sea, and air. Missing from all the breakthroughs that can be so easily commodified at exponentially increasing rates, is anything to do with the human behaviors and costs to society that result from poverty, ignorance and crime. all of which continue to jam up our judicial systems, fill our jails, and in so many ways diminish, squander and threaten our collective potential. This is the 75 percent reality that can only be addressed by a more comprehensive commitment to a behavioral-centered sense of design.

The future is unfolding in ways that will make our technological inventions seem increasingly miraculous. Against this background, and as a way to help keep us focused on the far more significant need to advance the human art of creative relationships, consider this simple description of a cartoon which crystallizes the limitations of technology.

The drawing shows the only two charred twigs left standing against a background of the still-smoldering ruins of earth, a scene that could only result from the extraordinary power of technology. An amoeba clinging to one of the twigs, says to an amoeba on the other – "Next time we leave out the brain."

OWNERSHIP & STEWARDSHIP

And God blessed them, and God said unto them, Be fruitful, and multiply, and replenish the earth, and subdue it: and have dominion over the fish of the sea, and over the fowl of the air, and over every living thing that moveth upon the earth."

–Genesis 1:28

One can only assume that the writer of Genesis envisioned a somewhat different outcome as a result of our subduing the earth and holding dominion over all living things. This would seem especially true given the imperceptibly short amount of time we have had to leave our mark on the earth compared to the geologic expanse of the Creation.

"In the 24 hours since this time yesterday, over 200,000 acres of the rainforest have been destroyed in our world. Fully 13 million tons of toxic chemicals have been released into our environment. Over 45,000 people have died of starvation, 38,000 of them children. And more than 130 plant or animal species have been driven to extinction by the actions of humans. (The last time there was such a rapid loss of species was when the dinosaurs vanished.) And all this just since yesterday."[1]

"Global freshwater consumption rose more than sixfold last century. Water tables are falling due to our over-pumping of ground water — for example, withdrawals from the Ogallala aquifer in the U.S. are three times the recharge rate. Many rivers, such as Amu Dar'ya, Colorado, Ganges, Indus, Rio Grande, and Yellow, run dry for part of the year."[2]

"Although we live in a highly urbanized, technologically advanced society, we are as dependent on the earth's natural support systems as the Sumerians and Mayans were. If we continue with business as usual, civilization collapse is no longer a matter of whether but when. We now have an economy that is destroying its natural support systems, one that has put us on a decline and collapse path."[3]

As for taking dominion over the fish of the sea, the fowl of the air, and "every living thing that moveth upon the earth," we've got that covered as well. "Unwittingly for the most part, but right around the world, we are eliminating the panoply of life. We elbow species off the planet, we deny room to entire communities of nature, we domesticate the Earth. With growing energy and ingenuity, we surpass ourselves time and again in our efforts to exert dominion over the fowl of the air and fish of the sea...Eventually we may achieve our aim, by eliminating every 'competitor' for living space on the crowded Earth. When the last creature has been accounted for, we shall have made ourselves masters of all creation. We shall look around, and we shall see nothing but each other. Alone at last."[4]

Ideas and the Land

Buckminster Fuller, by a combination of his prophecies and his living example, sets forth our paradoxical reasoning when it comes to ownership. In frequent and varied ways he would both suggest and prophesy that "one idea could feed the world." This would seem to imply, for example, that Facebook, instead of making Mr. Zuckerberg a multibillionaire as a result of his patented ideas, his invention would result in sharing those billions with the citizens of the world.

For those of us who were born into a society that takes the ownership of land not only as a given but as something associated with care and responsibility, it can be unsettling to realize or be reminded of the voices who regarded it to be a travesty. Jean-Jacques Rousseau in his 1775, *Discourse of the Origin of Inequality* first seems to favor the civilizing influence of property rights then condemns it as though it were the source of all human suffering.

> "The true founder of civil society was the first man who, having enclosed a piece of land, thought of saying, 'This is mine,' and came across people simple enough to believe him. How many crimes, wars, murders, and how much misery and horror the human race might have been spared if someone had pulled up the stakes or filled the ditch, and cried out to his fellows: 'Beware of listening to this charlatan. You are lost if you forget that the fruits of the earth belong to all and that the earth itself belongs to no one."[5]

The same conflict could be associated with Adam Smith, a darling of capitalism on one hand, but not so with respect to the ownership of property, which he saw as a kind of war by the rich waged against the poor. "Civil government, so far as it is instituted for the security of property, is in reality an institute for the defense of the rich against the poor, or of those who have some property against those who have none at all."[6]

Henry George, was an egalitarian theorist whose 1879 *Progress and Poverty* argued against ownership of land, just as we might argue against the private ownership of air. Because in both cases, no private interests had created either, thus they are as something to be shared. This lead others like Ambrose Bierce to suggest that the private ownership of land, which inevitably restricts its access, is tantamount to saying that only people who own land have a right to live. [7]

In his classic *Sand County Almanac*, Aldo Leopold, one of this nation's most revered ecologists, opposed the ownership of land but for a very different reason. "We abuse the land because we regard it as a commodity belonging to us. When we see land as a community to which we belong, we may begin to use it with love and respect...conservation is a state of harmony between men and land."[8]

Faced with the wisdom and logic of Rousseau, Adam Smith, Henry George, Ambrose Bierce and Aldo Leopold, is there something to be learned from the living example of a billion people, soon to be billions, who hold a very different view that we might want to study, or is this simply beyond our present reality?

Robert Neuwirth takes us back to an earlier time. "Land was not born as property. Property is a human creation and only one way of organizing the world. Before the system of privately held property became prevalent, people used to have a right that was so basic, so inextricably tied to living that no one thought to codify it."

That was then and this is now. The 21st century demands a more fine grained view that goes beyond simply being for or against the ownership of land. There is land, which may be "owned" in theory, but if so it exists more like an abandoned child. With reference to Aldo Leopold, such property is neither loved nor respected and is certainly not "in a state of harmony between men and land." Can this disgrace be chalked up to the fact that the land is owned? Hardly. Consider this very different example of ownership.

The story is told of a local preacher visiting a farm owned by one of his parishioners. Being obviously impressed with the cultivated beauty of the farmer's fields, extending as far as he could see, the preacher placed his hand on the farmer's shoulder, and in a kind of prayerful whisper, said, "I can't imagine any more beautiful land than what I see here that you and God have created together." The farmer thought for a moment, then shook his head, replying, "But pastor – you should have seen what this land looked like when God had it all by himself."

Values and Stewardship

With this background and given that the pursuit of community is as much as possible, the win/win opposite to the mutual devastation of war, it is critically important to address the rights, values and stewardship associated with the ownership of land. In our attempt to do so, even the wisdom of Solomon may not be sufficient.

We could side with those who say, since none of us created the land, none of us can own it. And if we were to purchase it, from whom would we get the invoice? The same issues could arise with respect to other things we didn't create, for example, air, water, photosynthesis, and all the earth's minerals, vegetation, and wildlife. We might also be against the ownership of land remembering that, by way of slavery, respectable people, even those among the founders of this country, once thought it proper to own people.

At the same time there can be no disagreement when acknowledging that humans cannot exist without the spoils of the earth nor some form of agreed-upon allegiance to law. To this we must add that the greatest variable of all is that which results from our values. Richard Farson, a brilliant thinker, author and friend puts the connection between law, values and behavior, most bluntly. "We'll never get rid of our crime problem because it's too close to our value system." That element of our value system to which he refers is most easily summarized as, *get all you can in the most expedient way possible, no matter who it may hurt.* Even if this approach could stand the basic test of being legal, it will never cross the higher hurdle of being artful and certainly not sustainable.

Trapped by What We've Achieved

Marshall McLuhan, a professor at Canada's McGill University became famous for coining phrases like, "The medium is the message." One of my favorites was McLuhan's twist on Shakespeare, which he offered as,

"To the *spoils* belong the *victor*." A dramatic example of this occurred following a meeting with one of Mexico's billionaires. The meeting took place in the penthouse of his highrise office building in Mexico City. Our session was planned to include a visit to a compound his foundation had created for the benefit of the city's children.

From my host's lavish offices, we walked up a flight of steps to the roof of the building where we boarded his French, turbine-driven helicopter. As we began our forward ascent, crossing over the edge of the roof, I was ready for the vastness of the city, but not for the gray blanket of smog that extended in all directions as far as I could see. Wanting to provoke some response from my host, I simply asked, "Do you like living in Mexico City?' To which he answered with a question of his own, "Aren't we all kind of trapped by what we've achieved?"

Stewardship Beyond Ownership

By now, anything concerning the ownership of land has been addressed by centuries of laws, treaties and war, all spelled out by way of various legal documents, some current and well established, others historic and contested. In addition to private ownership, we have public lands, tribal lands held in trust, land owned in common by direct agreement and that owned by way of non-profit foundations. Along with all of this we've had range wars, and we still have land fraud. Most interesting of all are the informal agreements between individuals and groups that "govern" the leasing, buying and selling of land for which none of the participants have any form of legal ownership. This "field research" is the everyday reality for the more than a billion and growing number of individuals and families, living and working as citizens of the third world's so-called squatter cities.

If Aldo Leopold's opposition to the ownership of land could have been looked at a little closer he might have been willing to make a distinction between those who use, but also value and care for the land for its own sake, as opposed to those, (to use his own words,) "treat it as a commodity to be bought and sold." The latter was epitomized by the head of a home building company when he said that he was not really in the business of building houses, "I just put them on the land as a way to increase its value."

In his 1943 autobiography, under the heading of "Land," Frank Lloyd Wright wrote, "Thanks to provisions of government, great natural and National Parks are becoming everywhere available for recreation." In a sense, Wright created two of his own "national parks" by way of Taliesin and Taliesin West, both Registered National Landmarks, now toured by visitors from all over the world.

Wright and his Welsh ancestors before him settled in the south central portion of Wisconsin known as "The Driftless Region." This is a heavily wounded area of hills and valleys left in their present state because they were outside the path of the great glaciers that passed through and leveled the countryside. Wright was both a steward and assembler of the land which he clearly loved. At one point the Taliesin estate included more than 5,000 acres of farmlands and preserved woodlands which he cared for with the same attention and artistry that he gave to the design and care of his buildings.

Returning to Genesis 1:28 in which God seems to instruct Adam and Eve to subdue the earth, E.O. Wilson offers this more positive understanding. "Once in history this passage was construed to validate the conversion of nature to exclusively human needs. Now it is more commonly interpreted to mean the stewardship of nature." Patriarch Bartholomew I, spiritual leader of the world's 250 million Orthodox Christians, has declared, in the clarion tones of an Old Testament prophet, that for humans to cause species to become extinct and to destroy the biological diversity of God's creation, for humans to degrade the integrity of the earth by causing changes in its climate, by stripping the earth of its natural forests, or destroying its wetlands, for humans to contaminate the earth's waters, its land, its air and its life with poisonous substances, these are sins."[9] Imagine what a different experience we would share if all the world's religions inspired and demanded this sense of stewardship for the land on which all of life depends.

THE ANATOMY OF PEACE

"The vision of a world community based on justice, not power,
is the necessity of our age...the test of policy is how it ends, not how it begins."

–Henry A. Kissinger

Nicholas Murray Butler became president of Columbia University in 1902 and received the Nobel Prize in 1932. He was a brilliant and witty man who would suggest to his students that at some point in the Garden of Eden, Adam must have looked at Eve and said, "I just can't stop thinking that we are living at a time of transition." Not only would Adam's "feelings" have been well-founded, his imagined sense of the future has been in the process of accelerating ever since.

Henry Kissinger's words would have had no meaning for most of human history when dispersed gatherings of individuals and groups existed all over the earth with little or no knowledge of anyone's presence but their own. Adam's imagined words to Eve anticipated that this wouldn't always be the case. The Jesuit priest Teilhard de Chardin put it all together: "God made the world round so that one day we would have to confront each other." It was that "one day" that prompted Emery Reves in 1945 to write, *The Anatomy of Peace* in which he set forth a scenario of the unending local to global conflicts and wars that would result from independent nation states existing in ever-closer contact with no shared rules to govern their relationships. He compared this to the chaos that would inevitably erupt between our then 48 states had there been no overriding rules of governance for addressing their individual desires and differences.

Reves dedicated *The Anatomy of Peace* to his Mother who was, "atrociously and senselessly assasinated, like countless other innocent victims of the war whose martyrdom can have meaning only if we who survive learn how to prevent the tragedy of future wars." The first third of his book is a detailed account of the necessity for the "vision of a world community based on justice, not power." This was the same achievement that Kissinger was to call for well over a half century later. An inability to achieve this, according to Reves, would result in the failure of capitalism, socialism, and religion, placing the world's people on the road to facism. He gave an account of how, in spite of the Monroe Doctrine and our desire to remain aloof from Europe, in 1917 we were *forced* to enter the first World War. After describing how essential and righteous this was, as seen from the position of the United States, he provides what everything seemed like at the time when viewed from the perspective of the British Isles. This was followed by describing the war as seen by the citizens of France, then Germany and Moscow. When viewed from their respective interests, there were no aggressors. This lead to Reves' most basic of all conclusions:

> "There is not the slightest hope that we can possibly
> solve any of our vital problems until we rise above dogmatic
> nation-centric conceptions and realize that, in order to
> understand the political, economic and social problems
> of this highly integrated and industrialized world, we
> have to shift our standpoint and see all the nations
> and national matters in motion, in their interrelated
> functions, rotating according to the same laws without
> any fixed points created by our own imagination for our
> own convenience."[1]

Rather than seeing this as anything radical, he is simply stating that striving for peace requires what our own Alexander Hamilton wrote in his Federalist paper No. 6: "To look for a continuation of harmony between a number of independent, unconnected sovereignties, situated in the same neighborhood, would be to disregard the uniform course of human events, and to set at defiance the accumulated experience of the ages."

Given the state of the 21st century world, at least as characterized by the 24/7 flow of news, it would certainly seem to preclude Reve's path to peace. To paraphrase his arguments, the reason Illinois doesn't launch rockets into Wisconsin is that both states understand they are governed by a common law that would make such an attack counterproductive.

In an effort to reduce the innumerable variables of war to their most basic causes, Reves' cites two of what he calls the most "unmistakable observations". Wars between groups of men forming social units always take place when these units, be they tribes, dynasties, religions, cities, or nations, exercise unrestricted sovereign power. And wars between these social units cease the moment sovereign power is transferred from them to a benign and higher unit.

A Growing Awareness

Given all that has occurred during the almost seven decades since the observations in *The Anatomy of Peace*, there have been three major changes. While we may not all be connected in our doctrinal beliefs, our ever-closer global proximities coupled with the connectedness of our atmosphere, oceans, rivers, and streams has brought us into a one-world awareness. This new and growing focus with respect to sustainability moves all of us closer to being on the same page. The second observation is that weapons which once took the strength of a nation to deliver can now be deployed by individuals or groups. For all manner of reasons, we're becoming less impressed with what the bureaucracy's of government can accomplish while becoming more aware of the seeming miracles of both nature and technology. The third change is that since 1945 the number of individual nations has more than tripled from 60 to 196.

In the last 10,000 years, humans have come to dominate our planetary home. We now know that the technologies that we have invented to suit our needs, are now the same technologies that have the power to poison or destroy paradise. So real is this threat that Stephen Hawking, referring to the fragility of earth has said, "We would be wise to keep our eggs in as many baskets as possible."

Hawking's advice might be considered to be nothing but good sense in terms of exploring our options. However, the spirit of keeping one's options open would probably not be the best way of contributing to one's community any more than keeping one's options open would likely result in a rewarding and productive marriage. As for our planetary home, an option that we might want to keep open was expressed by Václav Havel:

> "The salvation of this human world lies nowhere else than in the human heart, in the human power to reflect, in human meekness and human responsibility. Without a global resolution in human consciousness nothing will change for the better and the catastrophe towards which this world is headed will be unavoidable."[2]

We've all heard the argument that suggests how quickly the nation's of the world would unite if, all of a sudden we were being invaded by an unknown and powerful species from outer space. In response to this, Emery Reves writes, "We would forget all our ridiculous international quarrels and would willingly and gladly place ourselves under one rule of law for sheer survival."

Might we eventually come to acknowledge that, without invaders from space, we live daily with a common enemy. Fortunately this multi-headed "enemy" is getting our attention as never before. In the simplest possible terms our common enemy is the difference between our understanding of what we call the market, combined with our relative ignorance and abuse of the more holistic, life-maintaining, beauty and eco-system services of nature.

Adjusting to Change

In 1988, Paul Kennedy wrote the *Rise and Fall of The Great Powers*, which became an international bestseller. This was followed five years later by his *Preparing for the Twenty-First Century* in which he examines the affects of global connections, including the increased power and tension brought about by instant communication.

Addressing what he calls, "The American Dilemma," he uses a series of comparisons to chart American's historic strengthening followed by what he saw in 1993 as its emerging weakening. Most, if not all of these indicators have continued to worsen ever since. Kennedy's advice for Americans is to ignore all the changes we may not like but are irrevocably in motion while focusing on that which we can do best.

We are gradually relearning what has always been true. No matter how insignificant any one of us may feel compared to the giantism of governments and corporations, we can no longer look to either to address our most significant hurdles or dreams. Despite living at a time of massively organized programs, the success of our human future is not to be found in the hands of great powers. It will come from the civility and creativity of individuals living and working with unbounded dedication for doing things a better way.

Governments are empowered to pass laws and fund projects, but they have little or no power to make humanity creative and caring. Corporations can invest in ever more complex pharmaceuticals along with unprecedented technologies for diagnostic and related treatment but they can't make us healthy. To be caring, creative, and healthy will always require individual intention and commitment.

Will humanity learn how to live to be hundreds of years old, or even invent ways to live forever, as some now believe? Even if this were to be a possibility it would be best to think of it more as a detail than anything relating to our success or failure as humans. This is not to minimize whatever unknowable accomplishments may lie ahead, but rather to acknowledge that behavioral progress is far more difficult to achieve than even our most exciting and far- reaching inventions. Evidence of this is that among our brightest and best are those who predict that the 21st Century will include WWIII. If this occurs, it would indicate that despite the continuous roll-out of technological progress there has been little or no progress on the side of our behaviors.

The Turning Point

Such dismal thinking assumes that we will never reach a human balance that can stand on its own without the strong taking advantage of the weak. Might the energy and futility of destroying each other simply run out of steam? Or will humanity continue its war of ignorance, not only against itself but against nature, to which nature's response becomes our common enemy. This being a war no group or nation could win, might it result with all of us being on the same side, maybe even coming to our senses on time to become partners in creation?

We might awaken to the fact that what we think of as the beauty of nature is inseparable from its life-renewing technologies. Might this then lead us toward an integrated understanding of all human inventions including governance, education, religion, and the systems of financial exchange? Might we learn to value the uncertainties and explorations of the arts more, and the certainties of doctrine and argument less? Might health become more about living than curing, and more general than special?

Buckminster Fuller never missed a chance to point out that nature has no special departments for physics, chemistry, biology or religion. As we contemplate Bucky's *Utopia or Oblivion*, and in this spirit of the unity of nature, might we one day awaken to the unity of our human nature? Might it be that nature also has no separate departments for the variety of beliefs we hold that can so easily threaten everyone's future?

If we can't approach the anatomy of peace any other way, we might at least admit and share three observations that have not the slightest chance of being wrong.

1. The first is that there has never been, nor will there ever be, a war to end all wars, unless of course, we succeed in the mutual annihilation of everyone.

2. The second is that technology's geometrically increasing power to destroy, coupled with its ever-increasing miniaturization gives individuals the power, that in the past could only be unleashed by the world's superpowers.

3. Lastly, failure to heed the warning of the first two observations will find us on the wrong side of Fuller's Utopia or Oblivion.

A good and powerful first step back from the brink of disaster would be to accept that however we may think of the difficulties to be encountered in pursuing the art of community, it has a different and far better outcome that the easier to imagine destructive force of war.

It should be obvious to all that the future of American success is in for its greatest retooling since that which emerged from WWII. The most effective way to face the future is neither with crippling pessimism nor naïve optimism. What the future requires from every one of us who has the capacity to contribute, is to be both open and innovative in seeking new avenues empowered by our own and individual reasons for hope.

The second decade of the 21st century represents a kaleidoscopic collision of values. The world's great religions are in conflict with both governments and each other. We are not surprised by the fall of long-standing dictators. We see both deeper into the world of quantum physics and further out into the relativities of time and space. We use ever-smaller devices to accomplish ever-greater tasks, all well beyond the once clear cause and effect of the technologies of our past. We've extended the influence of individual will, giving human decisions the equivalent of eternal life, all by way of the legal structures of corporations and foundations. We've blurred the lines between debt and equity and reduced the life-cycle of "ownership" to milliseconds by way of algorithmic investing.

Fragmentation takes the form of massive bureaucracies, political parties, professions, and global communication networks, all using dazzling sounds and images to mask the too often superficialities of what they promise to deliver.

The more esoteric our pursuits, the more impossible it seems to communicate between an extraordinary array of intellectual disciplines including physics, mathematics, biology, psychology, science and the arts. Also, not so easy to communicate are the cost/benefit ratios between short and long range implications, for example the per capita appropriations for incarceration versus one-tenth the per capita amount expended for education, or to rationalize the short-term spurts of profit in one area causing exponentially greater, long-term losses in another. Nowhere is this more obvious than in the cost of both war and the threat of war.

In the words of Dwight D. Eisenhower, who was first a five-star general before he became president, "Every gun that is made, every warship launched, every rocket signifies, in the final sense, a theft from those who hunger and are not fed, from those who are cold and are not clothed. The world in arms is not spending money alone. It is spending the sweat of its laborers, the genius of its scientists, the hopes of its children."

What unites the warnings of Emery Reves, President Eisenhower, and the much later advocacy of Henry Kissinger, is beyond politics. It is simply the long overdue realization that the nations of the world, each in their own way, will one day have to observe that we've made war both unaffordable and obsolete. To put it in the context of this book, notwithstanding all the ever-more ingenious ways that it is waged, war is extremely deficient design. Consider for example, its affect on our national treasury. In 2007 the "United States borrowed more than $740 billion from the rest of the world...which translates to $1.4 million every second."[3] How is all this money spent? Under the heading of "Global Governance," the following itemization of costs is from *The New GAIA Atlas of Planet Management.*

"As of late 2004 the Iraq War cost the U.S. $150 billion. The same $150 billion could have provided health care for 82 million American children. At the global level the $150 billion could have halved world hunger as well as supplied HIV/AIDS vaccines, childhood immunization and clean water/sanitation for the developing world for more than two years. A single Cruise Missile costs $800,000; 320 were launched at Baghdad. The U.S. has also spent at least $50 billion on military activities in Afghanistan. Rebuilding Iraq could cost $50-75 billion."

Count out 60 seconds, and three of the world's children have died for lack of safe water/sanitation. Count out another 60 seconds, and within these two minutes the world would have spent $3.4 million on its military. Indeed, we are currently spending $880 billion a year on instruments of death – and, in the process, opening up a new battlefield of social neglect. Between 1945 and 2000, at least 50 million lives were lost in war and other forms of violent conflict. In 2004, the U.S. budgeted one dollar of aid for every $19 in defense. Between 2000 and 2005, the U.S. will have spent roughly $2.2 trillion on military activities. The tragedy is that sustainable economic development could remove many pre-war tensions."

If there was any other choice, no thinking person would ever knowingly endorse the continuation of this tragedy, some motivated by logic, others by something far deeper.

Living in Two Worlds

In one world, our military ability for attack and defense is a self-evident necessity for survival. The other world has been summed up by E.O. Wilson juxtaposing our "god-like technology" with our "stone age emotion and medieval self-image".

The most interactive and dominant two-worlds experiences, include the goals of our market-based economy and the broader needs of life itself. As brutal and mindless as it sometimes seems, a market-driven economy makes it possible to live in democratic freedom. As the Nobel-winning economist Milton Friedman said, "the only social responsibility of business is to make a profit."[5]

The other world relies on the design-based professions in general, and the non-profits in particular, all as set forth in the introduction: "The more we move from the world of design to the design of the world, the more empowered we will become to provide for the yet-unborn who will either suffer or thrive as a result of what and how we plan for their arrival." To repeat Frank Lloyd Wright's imagined words, "the client is the future, the programs are those birthed in the visions of the designer, and among the most important initiatives are those for which there will be no one to send the invoice."

Perhaps the most basic of our two worlds is that of male and female as addressed in Riane Eisler's, *The Chalice and the Blade*, which Ashley Montague called the most important book since Darwin's, *Origin of Species*. Listen as Eisler puzzles her way through an age-old question.

"Why do we hunt and persecute each other? Why is our world so full of man's infamous inhumanity to man – and to woman? How can human beings be so brutal to their own kind? What is it that chronically tilts us toward cruelty rather than kindness, toward war rather than peace, toward destruction rather than actualization?

Of all life-forms on this planet, only we can plant and harvest fields, compose poetry and music, seek truth and justice, teach a child to read and write – or even laugh and cry. Because of our unique ability to imagine new realities and realize these through ever more advanced technologies, we are quite literally partners in our evolution. And yet, this same wondrous species of ours now seems bent on putting an end not only to its own evolution but to that of most life on our globe, threatening our planet with ecological catastrophe or nuclear annihilation."[6]

"One of the most striking things about Neolithic art is what it does not depict. For what people do not depict in their art can tell us as much about them as what they do...a theme notable for its absence from Neolithic art is imagery idealizing armed might, cruelty, and violence-based power. There are no images of 'noble warriors' or scenes of battles. Nor are there any signs of 'heroic conquerors' dragging captives around in chains or other evidences of slavery.

Also in sharp contrast to the remains of even the earliest and most primitive male-dominant invaders, what is notable in these Neolithic Goddess-worshipping societies is the absence of lavish 'chieftain' burials. And in marked contrast to later male-dominant civilizations like that of Egypt, there is here no sign of mighty rulers who take with them into the afterlife less powerful humans sacrificed at their death."[7]

"This theme of the unity of all things in nature, as personified by the Goddess, seems to permeate Neolithic art. For here the supreme power governing the universe is a divine Mother who gives her people life, providing them with material and spiritual nurturance, and who even in death can be counted on to take her children back into her cosmic womb."[8]

Eisler quotes from the edition of the *World Military and Social Expenditures* report that came out about the time she was writing *The Chalice and the Blade*.

"The cost of developing one intercontinental ballistic missile could feed 50 million children, build 160,000 schools, and open 340,000 health care centers. Even the cost of a single new nuclear submarine – equal to the annual education budget of twenty-three developing countries in a world where 120 million children have no school they can go to and 11 million babies die before their first birthday – could open new opportunities for millions of people now doomed to live in poverty and ignorance."[9]

Both the above report by Ruth Sivard and that which follows by Elizabeth McLeod go well beyond anything that can be so neatly accounted for in the fragmentation of metrics we call "the bottom line."

"I believe if women ruled the world, we could all learn from an early age that the job of every human being is to improve the Earth. There would not be wars and bombings of innocent people. Women know what it means when the news says, "Two people were killed in Iraq." They can imagine how the mother felt to have her miracle destroyed. That is what war is, when you think about it: destruction of the millions of miracles women have made.

It takes about 8.25 years of a woman's actual physical labor to raise an 18-year-old person. A child takes 100 percent of the mother's time the first two years, 50 percent of her time the next six years, and about 25 percent of her time from the ages 9 to 18, for a total of 8.25 years of labor. Multiply 8.25 by the thousands killed in war, and you have billions of years of actual women's labor put to waste in one war. You see, women get that number and shake their heads in disgust. They know the value of those years and the pain of the next 50 years, living with a broken heart."[10]

As Viewed from the 21st Century

Considering the nearly seven decades of events that have been added to the historic record since the publishing of *The Anatomy of Peace*, we should be in a far better position than its author to evaluate his thesis. His most basic of all observations has two parts. The first is that technology has brought the world's people into a geometrically increasing proximity and awareness. The second is that this has occurred with no preparation for making this a peaceful transition. Reves would say that the first is symbolized by our two world wars and the global economy that followed. The second observation, inseparable from the first, is that the closer, more familiar and more linked the world's people become without any shared governance, the greater the likelihood for ongoing violence and losses resulting from all manner of conflict. Reves makes the argument that organizations like the United Nations, for all the good they might do in terms of facilitating dialogue, they are nonetheless powerless, and maybe even harmful, in that they increase the awareness of warring interests with neither the ability nor the mandate to stop violence wherever it may erupt.

Those of us who live in the United States will inevitably view the world from our own special vantage point. Consider, for example, this 2005 description of American Power. " Americans are members of a country that possesses power – whether economic, technological, military – to affect the entire world to a degree undreamed of by Alexander the Great, Julius Caesar, Napoleon, or Stalin. Yet four out of five Americans have never held a passport. Do they realize that yesterday's world is made to look truly ancient by today's globalization?"[11]

The same man who chronicled the preceding observation, also wrote this. "When I, Norman Meyers, go the airport, I reflect that the bit of cardboard in my hand, known as a passport, is a hangover from a former age. Although I have lived and worked in a world of 200 management packages that we call nations, it is increasingly one indivisible world – a continuum of economies, environments, politics, cultures, and security. We are no longer just Americans or Britishers, we are also card-carrying citizens of a single global community. The fossil-fuel pollution of the aeroplane I fly in and the global warming it generates mean I am much more than a Britisher."[12]

To those of us who were born into the freedom-enabling benefits of the United States Constitution which has also been a lifeline for generations escaping oppression from elsewhere, the idea of some form of global governance may not only seem undesirable, but threatening in the extreme.

The second and equally obvious area of concern is the tendency for centralized governance to incrementally and systematically move toward increasing its own power and control. The more the world moves away from local, highly self-sufficient communities, the greater the potential to manipulate the worldwide system for dominance. To address all this, we would need a 21st century version of the miracle pulled off by our founding "fathers," only this time the world may be better, more comprehensively served if in the hands of its founding "mothers."

TALIESIN
Spring Green, Wisconsin

TALIESIN WEST
Scottsdale, Arizona

The Master and His Apprentices
Vernon Swaback is on his left in both of the lower images

FRANK LLOYD WRIGHT'S UNFINISHED WORK

"I'll probably die with my work half done"

–Frank Lloyd Wright

Autumn at Taliesin in Wisconsin always occasioned the need to start thinking about our annual pilgrimage across the country to Taliesin West in the Sonoran desert. While we all looked forward to being in Arizona, it was always bittersweet. Wisconsin in the Fall is a celebration of the sumac bushes turning their special bright red, the multi-colored oaks and especially the maple trees, all ablaze in their customary reds, oranges and yellows. Add to this that Wisconsin's Fall atmosphere is crisply intoxicating.

It was on a Sunday like this in 1958 that Wright began his customary talk to the apprentices; " The time has come for us to pack up and leave for the desert. As always, we're leaving here with our work half done. I'll probably die with my work half done." That thought carried little concern for us. Wright always seemed so youthful, that no matter his age, in some less than logical way, it was possible to think of him as outliving all of us. This thought was reinforced by his actions along with statements like, "Age! I can't do anything about that – but youth! That's a quality."

Before six months had passed, his prophecy of leaving his work half finished became a reality. In the second week of the following April, he was taken to a hospital in Phoenix to be treated for what was thought to be a minor matter but there were complications. He left us on Saturday, April 9, 1959. In the months and years that followed, life went on for those of us who were both resident members of the Taliesin Fellowship and staff of the "Office of Frank Lloyd Wright." This name eventually changed to the *Taliesin Associated Architects, a subsidiary of the Frank Lloyd Wright Foundation.*

Given that Wright died at the pinnacle of his career, the work in the office continued with the advantage of having a broad range of commissions including everything from custom residences and churches to New York's Guggenheim Museum, the Gammage Auditorium for Arizona State University and the Marin County Government Center in San Rafael, California, all soon followed by new commissions, including a series of fine art centers in Florida, Kentucky and California.

In addition to the work of the architectural office, two related circumstances provided for an uninterrupted continuation of life at both Taliesin and Taliesin West. Unlike the death of an individual that attracts friends and relatives to gather for a day or two, along with the many guests who did this, were the approximately 70 of us who constituted the live/work Taliesin Fellowship, all in residence and all carrying out our respective roles in both the professional practice and the activities of the community.

There was also an overall sense of continuity by way of the on-going leadership of Mrs. Wright, who was not only cofounder of the Taliesin Fellowship, but without her, it is unlikely that it would have been created. And if by some miracle it had, without her guidance it is doubtful that it could have persisted through the many challenges to be addressed during the three and a half decades prior to Wright's death. As long as she was present to reinforce and reinvigorate the always inspiring culture of the community, in a deeply felt sense, it seemed as though Wright was still there as well. This was a feeling I experienced for much of my time at Taliesin, and many years later when I was asked to serve as the Foundation's Chairman, it was that same sense of being inspired by his uncommon insights that made it all worthwhile.

The Half Wright "Finished"

This man who was born just two years after the Civil War in a remote Wisconsin town, broke away from the more prevalent imitative tendencies exemplified by Chicago's 1893 Columbian Exposition. In so doing, Wright sought to create a new architecture befitting our young country's declaration of the sovereignty of the individual. He lavished attention on modest, but brilliantly designed houses for school teachers, journalists, small business owners, and others that he referred to as "our typical best citizens." So amazing were these modest designs that they frequently got more attention from the international press than major buildings that were being completed during the same period.

While others were using steel as nothing more than a stronger version of wood, he took advantage of its tensile strength, resulting in the cantilevered forms that often characterized his designs. He pioneered the frameless use of large sheets of glass as well as the large open atrium spaces that are now everywhere present especially in hotel and resort applications. His early designs for the Guggenheim Museum, set off a flood of dramatic institutional buildings by others, some of which are more interesting in themselves than they are in serving their intended purpose.

Wright's work is inseparable from what others now take for granted, which he described in various ways, with phrases like; *the nature of materials, the marriage of structures with their settings* and everything to do with *the reality of the building not being found in its roof and walls, but in the space within to be lived in.* The 1956 design of his "Mile High Building," has inspired dramatic structures that now echo its forms, but so far have yet to reach half its height, including Dubai's amazing Burj Khalifa.

Lasting fame, in the best sense of the word, goes far beyond the fleeting attraction of celebrity to achieve a timeless allegiance with those who embody the essence of something we all want and need to know. Still we ask, why hasn't the interest in Wright's work been satiated? Why are there more books about him being written today than ever before? Why have so many of our great institution's wanted access to his archives, which are now housed at the Museum of Modern Art and the Avery Architecture and Fine Arts Library at Columbia University.

Considering the high praise and publicity accorded the many star architects who continue to build with ever-increasing grandeur all over the world, how is it that this lone architect who lived most of his life in remote, hard-to-reach places remains the singular, world-wide and iconic name in architecture? All this implies that his life and work represents something that we might want to be more interested in exploring, which brings us back to the questions raised by his words in the fall of 1958, "I'll probably die with my work half done." And when he said that if he were to have another 15 years he could create "a whole new architecture," he clearly was not suggesting anything to do with a new style. Furthermore I'm quite certain it would not be a new way to simply reap the benefit of doing more of what he pioneered even though he would now have a far more responsive audience then when he was breaking beyond the limits of conventionality. His work was eventually so thoroughly copied that he once asked, "How do you think it feels to see your own regurgitation everywhere you look?" I also don't believe Wright would be interested in out-performing the architects of the 21st century as he had during the prior two centuries. That battle had been won.

There is no question that Wright anticipated the fruits of what his influence would have on the architects of the future, including individuals like Richard Rogers and Norman Foster, who crossed the United States together visiting everything they could find of his work. Wright innovated and stretched the limits of the systems and materials of his time to their breaking point. In so doing, he clearly knew that 21st century materials and systems would emerge allowing others to not only catch up his with heroic use and demonstrations with concrete, glass and steel, but that it would open up whole new possibilities. Considering how thoroughly he had been influential, he might even feel and express a sense of pride in the best of his 21st century progeny. Consider, for example this insight from designer, Bruce Mau.

"We must extend design and stewardship to encompass all terrain. The new global city is now defined with zones of urban, suburban, rural, leisure and even 'natural' precincts – all managed, all part of a designed system...Architects have tended to build pieces of cities without regarding their relationship to the whole. But holistic thinking is exactly what we need if we're ever to develop the capacity to provide shelter on a global scale. It's clear that synthesis is not merely useful; it's critical"[1]

From the World of Design to the Design of the World

Frank Lloyd Wright made little distinction between designing for a paying client or designing in pursuit of his own more broadly felt ideas and commitments. In a way most enduring, it is this same sense of meaning that continues to bring generations of visitors from all over the world to tour both his Taliesin and Taliesin West.

The tours originally conducted by his apprentices charging a dollar per person are now given by docents who offer a range of tours costing from $24 to $60. What a good many of the visitors want to learn most of all is focused on the life of the Taliesin Community. Where did everyone come from? How long did they remain? How did the work get done? Where did the children go to school and how did everything from the architectural work and education, to the celebrated cultural life of the international community take place?

Because these questions and their respective answers are given meaning by way of the physical structures that clearly convey a sense of life purpose, no one asks, for example, how much did the Pavilion cost, or why don't any of these doors have locks on them or why does an architectural office need two 150 seat theaters?

The Creative Community

Construction, architecture, pottery, cooking, and social activities were all part of the Taliesin day. While no single example will ever represent the perfect model for others, the central idea of a creatively integrated community is to provide the tools, settings and opportunities that facilitate the ability to remain engaged in rewarding activities throughout all ages and stages of life.

Some visitors ask, "It's a school, right? Then why have some of the students been here for decades?" And when they enter the Pavilion, they see an idea inscribed on a gold wall attributed to Laotze, the Chinese philosopher who lived 500 years before Christ. This already-referenced insight was central to Wright's approach "The reality of the building does not consist of its roof and walls, but in the space within to be lived in." The visitors are not only touching and seeing the artifacts of architecture, what makes it all so special is that they are sensing the space and spirit of community. Other than to simply get away for a time of relaxation and play, the places people want to visit most are those that convey a sense of working in very special ways for those who call it home.

The Art of Community

Frank Lloyd Wright could not have been any more successful in the design of memorable buildings than what he achieved in Japan with his design for the Imperial Hotel, one of the only structures to withstand Tokyo's great Kanto earthquake, or his design for "Fallingwater," very likely the most photographed house in the world or New York's Guggenheim, which launched, as we have said, a whole new approach to the design of museums and many other forms of public buildings.

Because he was far less successful in mainstreaming his approach to the art of community, notwithstanding his extraordinary commitment in this direction, for all the reasons stated, I not only believe this would be what he would consider his unfinished work, but for the future of humanity there is no pursuit where he could have contributed more.

Near the end of his life he said of his designs, that "he could now shake them out of his sleeve," which he clearly demonstrated on behalf of enabling clients, with their inspiring programs and beautiful sites. For anyone who wishes to apply that same commitment to the art of community as Wright did with his Broadacre City, the only enabling clients, inspiring programs and beautiful sites to be found are those that reside in the creative imagination of those who harbor the vision.

I witnessed Wright responding to a statement and at another time a question, liking neither. The statement occurred while he was, with his usual grace, showing a visitor one of his recent designs. The visitor quite obviously having understood nothing he had seen or heard, responded with, "Well, all it takes is money." Realizing the limitations of his guest, Wright said simply, "It might take a lot of money, but money alone won't do it."

The question that Wright had heard all too often was, "How does it feel to have ideas that are so far ahead of your time?" I would say he not only disliked, but hated the question. Answering with a somewhat aggressive tone he would say, "There's no such thing as being ahead of one's time. The time for idea to happen is just as soon as someone has it and commits to bringing it about." Related to this were the many occasions when he spoke of designing in ways that are "true to the time, the place, and the man."

Designing For A Cultural Way of Life

For most of the world's people, especially in the 21st century, "the time, the place, and the man," are always changing. This may be less so for those who can chart their own course by way of their financial position and in a very different way for those whose circumstances limit their range of possibilities. Four categories of changing societal dynamics can all be related to Wright's own inventive, artful and cultural way of life.

Family Formation: In earlier times, the extended family remained in place, if not for love and affection, there were the practical issues of circumstance which were often centered on two or three generations working the land, or in many instances of working for the same employer. Multi-generational stability was more the norm than anything exceptional.

According to the 2010 census, in 1950, only 22 percent of American adults were single. Today more than 44 percent of American adults are single, and 31 million – roughly one out of every three adults – lives alone. People who live alone make up 30 percent of all U.S. households, which makes them more common than any other domestic unit, including the nucelar family.[2]

How might Wright's focus on new environments and provisions for community be inspired by our current trajectory? For example during the first decade of this century, the U.S. population consisted of "92 million people who were unmarried or single, equivalent to 42 percent of all people over the age of 18. Of these, 60 percent had never been married, 25 percent were divorced, and 15 percent were widowed. Only a third of households had a child less than 18 years old (compared with half in 1960), and by 2025-30, this proportion may be no more than a fourth. The category of childless single people will continue to grow."[3] Rather than settling for the variety of special-purpose places designed for the retired and the elderly, we might more likely agree with the economic advisor who said, "The whole character, look, and feel of cities, neighborhoods, towns, and rural villages is likely to change..."[4]

The Changing Dynamics of Employment: Our increasingly one-world economy has relocated jobs that can be easily moved in search of the lowest cost providers. It is not surprising that what may be to the advantage of U.S. employers, has reduced and in some cases eliminated the corresponding jobs for the U.S. employees. A related pronouncement that preceded outsourcing by several decades, was made by Peter Drucker, one of the earliest and most revered prophets regarding all things relating to management. Drucker prophesized that the "largest employer of the future would one day be self." However else the future plays out, it takes no expert testimony to suggest that the once dominant position of the U.S. workforce that created this country's great middle class faces two new challenges. At one level while it is questionable if today's children are becoming as skilled as their parents, the opposite is true for what is taking place in countries like China and India. The resultant off-shoring of all manner of jobs has taken a toll on the once dominant U.S. work force. "Skilled blue-collar employees, the core of the traditional high-per-capita-income U.S. workforce have lost jobs in the millions as American firms wilted under international competition or relocated industrial production to other countries with lower labor costs."[5]

Related to this is the need to plan for all the issues related to the increasing longevity. One outcome could be a generational conflict regarding the tax-based distribution of wealth. A far better approach would be to design for a future which replaces the idea of retirement with life-long, sustaining engagement. We may not all agree with Ralph Waldo Emerson, but he had a point worth considering. He suggested that we would come to think of liesurely travel as a fools paradise, adding that places like Rome and Athens didn't get to be great because people went gadding about like moths around a candle flame, they got to be great because individuals stayed there and made them great. All these issues, properly considered, could not only lead to more satisfactory forms of community but also to new and more engaging forms of employment. Related to this are the multiple levels of cost associated with the time lost to commuting. According to the June 3, 2013 *New York Times*, "Commuters nearly double Manhattan's daytime population."

Collaborative consumption: What started with the timeshare use of cars, airplanes, vacation homes, tools and equipment, now extends to virtually every human provision and need. This is presented in fascinating detail in *What's Mine is Yours: The Rise of Collaborative Consumption*, including this summary, "The recent changes in our economic landscape have notably exposed and intensified a phenomenon: an explosion in sharing, bartering, lending, trading, renting, gifting, and swapping...organizations are redefining how goods and services are exchanged, valued, and created in areas as diverse as finance and travel, agriculture and technology, education and retail. Collaborative consumption may very well change the world."[6]

Occupant constructed settlements: There was a time, long, long ago, before the age of developers, before the invention of gas and electric powered machinery, before the existence of Home Depot and other building supply stores and before the dominance of corporations, codes and ordinances, when individuals had to rely on land they could access, materials they could find and ultimately their individual and shared skills and commitments to create where and how they lived. For more than a billion people, that one day is now.

The most studied evidence as to how these conditions are being addressed occur in what are called *Squatter Cities or Urban Slums.* Comprehensive insights into both their construction and way of life is provided in Robert Neuwirth's *Shadow Cities: A Billion Squatters, A New Urban World.*

As part of his research, Neuwirth, a student of philosophy, community organizer and reporter, committed to experience first-hand what he wanted to explore and document. Before it was all over, he lived in and experienced shantytowns on four continents, including settlements in Rio de Janeiro, Nairobi, Mumbai and Istanbul.

What makes his insights so informative is that he looks beyond what those who might quite reasonably see as the obvious problems. What Neuwirth conveys is a sense of the vitality and creativity of ordinary people who live not only without ownership, but also with little or no governmental assistance, and more often than not with a fair amount of on-going hostility. As a result he has found the deepest of reasons for extolling the virtues of ordinary people as they, by the harshest of necessities, pursue innovative ways, not only for surviving, but in some circumstances to actually prosper.

While it challenges our contemporary western values, one of the conditions that Neuwirth observes is that the inability to own land, has periodically been advocated as being of positive significance. Those of us for whom the ownership of land is somewhere close to godliness would be surprised by the response Neuwrith got to questioning the squatters as to how they would feel if the government offered them a title deed. In opposition to the idea, one respondent said, "It will never work. People will start fighting. So we will just have an exchange of grabbers, and the new grabbers will be us." Another suggested that, "a title deed would upset their amity, thus destroying the community in the name of helping it." [7]

By addressing a need that is not being handled any other way, the squatters are creating their own model and methods for a bartered way of building and living. The squatter populations are large and their numbers are likely to grow far faster than other segments of society. In the absence of any legal standing, they are pioneering a more basic, personal and human-based substitute for the far easier but now too limited availability of private ownership and the governance of law.

Squatter settlements come in all forms and densities. If the range of suggested statistics can be believed, Dharavi, shown above and featured in the film *Slumdog Millionaire,* has a density of 18,000 people per acre which would make it 166 times more dense than daytime Manhattan, with 85 percent of the people of Dharavi working where they live.

The top two images are typical of squatters settlements wherever they occur. The bottom hillside favela is in Rio de Janeiro.

The Frank Lloyd Wright Connection

How does all this relate to "The world's greatest architect? In many of the most obvious ways, it doesn't relate at all, but let's look a little deeper. Nearly eight decades ago when interstate roads didn't exist and cars weren't all that reliable and places to eat, sleep, or get service along the way were far and few between, Wright and his followers made the journey from Wisconsin to Arizona where neither persons nor places awaited their arrival.

Exposed to an essentially empty desert and with no other information than his own desires, Wright decided this was to be the winter location for the Taliesin Community. He found what would be considered today as Arizona's state land officer. When asked about the availability of property, the official's response was that he had a piece that he was "waiting for some fool to come along and fall in love with it." Wright said he thought he qualified.

Wright and his apprentices journeyed out to the site in the middle of the proverbial "nowhere." Not only were there no roads and no power, with respect to water Wright had been "guaranteed" that there would never be any. And for a man who cared about the "relatedness of all things", he certainly couldn't have known what might one day be built all around him, if anything.

Like today's squatters, whatever was to be built, Wright and his extended "family" would have to build themselves. Having precious little money to purchase materials, they dug up sand out of the natural desert washes and carried massive stones found at the base of the nearby mountains to use for the walls. The only materials to be purchased were cement to mix with the sand, rough sawn boards and rolls of canvas for the roofs. There was initially no plumbing, no electricity, thus no mechanical equipment of any kind, nor was there any glass. Only with time, coupled with an extraordinary amount of individual labor, were these provisions added, and only a piece at a time. Like today's squatters, anything needed, from the ground up, would have to be built by those who were making it their home.

Stewardship Without Ownership

Within four years of the start of this work, Frank Lloyd Wright not only transferred ownership of the land he purchased to a non-profit foundation, he, transferred all of his present and future earnings to the benefit of education. Individuals came to work and study from more than 25 nations, some remaining for their entire lifetime to be part of a society where there was neither visible nor behavioral differences between those who had no bank account and others who had great wealth. I often thought of Emerson's counsel that "a man must be so much as to make himself indifferent to circumstance."

In ways both simple and complex, the subjects of employment, family formation, collaborative consumption and constructing one's own habitats were more of an integrated and cultural lifestyle than anything to do with isolated specialties. In later years, visitors always seemed surprised to learn that this way of life which involved the most basic kinds of hand-built construction and daily self-maintenance would also involve twice-weekly formal black-tie dinners including presentations of live music and first run movies.

The photo shown below serves as a good illustration of the art of community in action. The individuals on the stage are rehearsing for what was Taliesin's Annual Festival of Music and Dance. The dance dramas were choreographed by Wright's daughter. The top of her head can be seen in the foreground of the photo sitting next to Mrs. Wright who composed the music. The musical score was orchestrated by Bruce Brooks Pfeiffer who was also the curatorial director of the Frank Lloyd Wright archives. The intricate costumes and ornamental headdresses were designed and fabricated by the dancer/architects. I am (unseen) in the orchestra pit as part of the Phoenix Symphony which performed under the direction of John Amarantides, another of the resident architects. As if this isn't sufficient evidence of a culturally diverse community, the dancers on stage are the same people who are both constructing the Pavilion, (shown partially completed) and also the architects who were working with Frank Lloyd Wright on the drawings for his proposed Arizona State Capital, all displayed on the easels shown in the photo against the back wall of the Pavilion.

Doing More With Less

What matters most for the future is not only the lessons to be found in Wright's extraordinary buildings but in the inventive demonstrations exemplified by his own way of life. He epitomized the meaning of the phrase, "when death finds you, may it find you fully alive." With all this in mind and with reference to Wright's unfinished work, consider some of the issues that can best, if not only, be addressed by an integrated way of life.

1. The 21st century's proximity of individuals representing widely divergent cultures and behaviors having little or no easy way to cultivate a common sense of purpose without engaging in some form of shared pursuits.

2. The comparative ease with which conventional society seems to understand the price of everything but finds it far more difficult to take the measure of anything more related to its long-term value.

3. The market-driven costs of specialty health care over the more holistic pursuits of a healthy way of living.

4. The degree to which we surrender our own creativity to the spectacle of everything from celebrity-worship to the packaging of news, movies and all other means that play on our fears or focus our attention somewhere outside anything to do with our own more creative sense of purpose.

5. Children growing up with no contact with nature as chronicled in; *Last Child in the Woods, Saving Our Children from Nature-Deficit Disorder*.

6. The high cost and waste of time and energy along with the air pollution and congestion caused by our daily back and forth commuting between where we live and where we work, study and play.

7. The all-too-frequent lack of any sense of shared community commitment beyond what we can lock and call our own.

8. Working for no other purpose than to earn a living.

9. An aging population combined with the loss of identity and purpose that can so easily result from so-called "retirement."

10. Treating "art" and "culture" as specialties divorced from our experiences of daily life.

11. The lack of any kind of natural surveillance where instead of cared-for communities, every house or apartment exists as its own unprotected island in a blur of sameness.

12. The lack of environmental beauty that so easily results from the demands and dominance of a market-driven economy.

Nothing could be both more futile and costly than to see any of these observations as being independent from the others, nor is there any way to easily bring them together other than by the challenging and innovative approaches for how we arrange for the needs and benefits of community. This challenging pursuit is what Frank Lloyd Wright was both developing and demonstrating by the special ways in which he conducted, shared, and celebrated his own long and productive life.

An Enduring Legacy

If all that the world knew and felt about Frank Lloyd Wright was to be found in his pioneering and dramatic approach to form and structure, he would have long since taken his place among other well-known architects of history but there is clearly much more to understand. More than a half century after his passing, during which architects have had the combined benefit of everything made possible by way of technological breakthroughs and unprecedented budgets, Wright's preeminence remains undiminished. Why is this? It certainly isn't just because he was clever, daring and dramatic. He was all that but there is far more. He was, of course, a great artist, but beyond all of this, he lives on as a kind of folk hero. His impact on all of us goes far beyond the design of his celebrated houses and buildings. Relating to the art of community, he would say, "Civilization is just a way of life. Culture is a way of making that way of life beautiful."

Designing Beyond What Isn't Working

Nothing seems to have become more standard for the observers of urban design and architecture than to praise the sustainable necessity of high-density cities. Wright had nothing against density, but what he abhorred was the wasteful, costly and unhealthy inefficiencies of crowding or what he more euphemistically referred to as "pig-piling" or "the trampling of the herd." To look beyond the simplistic notion that today's ever-larger cities are the wave of the future, consider the following three observations, each from a very different discipline.

Herbert Giradet is one of Britain's most prominent environmentalists. He is the Co-founder and Director of Programs for the World Future Council as well as an author and documentary filmmaker. Giradet has calculated London's "ecological footprint," by which he is referring to the reach beyond the city's own borders required to supply its needs and receive its wastes. He calculates this difference as being 293 times London's own surface area, to which he adds, "If every human being used resources the way we do in London, we would need three planets rather than the single one we have. Canadian, Australian and American cities have even larger foot-prints, extending to between eight and ten hectares of productive land per person. If everybody lived like Los Angelenos, we would need five planets."[8]

"Today's cities are consuming three-quarters of the world's energy and causing at least three-quarters of global pollution. They are the place of production and consumption of most industrial goods. Cities have become parasites on the landscape – huge organisms draining the world of their sustenance and energy: relentless consumers, relentless polluters...While in the developed world, city populations are effectively stagnating, in the developing world the multiple pressures of urban population explosion, economic development and migration from the countryside are expanding cities at a terrifying rate...a further two billion people are expected to be added to the cities of the developing world."[9]

The second insight is from demographer, George Magnus. He crystallizes something quite significant that can only be addressed by design. "Our presently dominant approach to urbanization, requires the harnessing of food, water, energy, and materials on a scale that is beyond nature..." He goes on to ask, "what do we do with the waste we generate in the form of the refuse, sewage, and pollution of air and water?" He then adds that we also "deliver cheap and processed food in a mass scale around the world," leading to "a global epidemic of obesity..."[10]

The third and final voice represents the perspective of a geographer. Harm de Blij is Distinguished Professor of Geography at Michigan State University. He offers this global perspective, which relates to our own U.S. debate concerning the future funding of social security; "According to a recent UN study, the Earth's total population by 2050 will approach nine billion. The (anticipated) 27 countries of the

European Union, however, will see their populations decline from 482 million to 454 million in 2050. Italy may drop from nearly 58 million to 45, Germany from 82 to 69, and if things do not change, to a mere 25 million by 2100. As Charlemagne writes in the July 19, 2003, issue of *The Economist*, 'Combine a shrinking population with rising life expectancy, and the economic and political consequences are alarming. In Europe there are currently 35 people of pensionable age per 100 people of working age. By 2050, on present demographic trends, there will be 75 pensionable for every 100 workers; in Spain and Italy the ratio of pensioners to workers is projected to be 1:1.' Because pensions are paid out of tax revenues, taxes will have to rise sharply to fund the generous pensions Europeans are accustomed to. Workers will demand that taxes be kept down, and labor unrest will become even more endemic in Europe than it already is. Further, countries with fairly stable populations, such as the Netherlands and the United Kingdom, will resent being enmeshed in the financial problems of other EU countries, creating potential schisms in the European Union."[11]

These three insights have only one thing in common. They may be addressed to some extent by technology or by some acceptable method of rethinking our present approach concerning cause and effect. But far more significantly, they are all issues relating to how we conceive of the relationships between us as individuals and the designed ideas for living and working together in community.

Seeing all this in light of Wright's own crusading way of life, it would follow that his view of the future would be that the most effective solutions to these and many other problems can only be achieved by way of new more integrated forms of how we live as individuals, how we live in relationships with each other, and how we design for our relatedness to the eco-system services of the earth.

If a man born just two years after the civil war, could so maintain our interest in his approach to a new urban form, based on the distance-collapsing invention of the motorcar, telephone and telegraph, imagine

Frank Lloyd Wright working on the Broadacre City model, a portion of which is shown to the right.

Land Uses

1. County seat
2. Airport
3. Stables and track
4. Sports fields
5. Baseball field
6. Athletic clubs
7. Lake and stream
8. Small farms
9. Custom residential
10. Interior parks
11. Music garden
12. Physical culture
13. Market center
14. Roadside center
15. Employee residential
16. Industry and dwellings
17. Commercial
18. Service businesses
19. Main parkway
20. Industry
21. Vineyards
22. Live/work
23. Residential
24. Schools

25. Worship center
26. Guest houses
27. Research center
28. Arboretum
29. Zoo
30. Aquarium
31. Country fair
32. Hotel
33. Country fair
34. Sanitarium
35. Industrial units
36. Medical clinics
37. Apartments
38. Dairy
39. Elementary school
40. Taliesin equivalent
41. Design center
42. Cinema
43. Forest cabins
44. Reservoir
45. Automobile objective
46. Garages and stores
47. Gas stations
48. Educational center

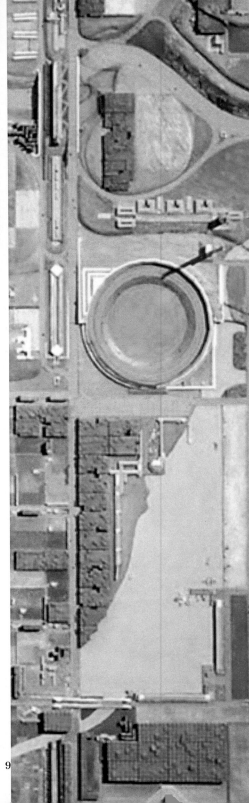

9

the yet to be envisioned breakthroughs for doing more with less when the special achievements of the digital technologies can be thoroughly integrated into the behavioral-centered fabric that helps to shape how and where we live.

When Humanity Becomes the Client

Wright's definition of "client" went far beyond the individuals and organization that commissioned his services. By way of his books and lectures he went further to address the more abstract, but very real to him, needs and aspirations of society, calling the general public, "our typical best citizens." Quoting again from *How Demographics are Changing the Global Economy and our World*, consider how Wright might respond to these further questions and observations.

"What will become of the role of the family in preparing young people for interaction in society if the family is comprised mainly of older relatives? Without siblings and peer age group relatives, how will children learn to offer and receive help and comfort as they do in bigger or extended families?...Family units without biological peers and comprising three, or possibly even four generations create different demands from more traditional ones...financial opportunities may be limited by lower economic growth, reduced retirement benefits, higher taxes, and the costs associated with retirement provisions..."[12]

However Wright would choose to respond, what we know for certain is that he crusaded and wrote four books, specifically addressing all these dynamics and more while investing 26 yeas of his life experimenting, refining and living out his own commitment to a multi-cultural, multi-generational integration of work, culture and creativity. On June 8, 1968, ten years after our first time together, in what was to be my last meeting with Buckminster Fuller, he described the live/work/study community that Frank Lloyd Wright created at Taliesin and Taliesin West as "An oasis of the regenerative spirit."

Wright would see what others might fear or think to be limitations as nothing but the basis for a whole new way of life, one as appropriate to the needs, limitations, and opportunities of the 21st century as his creative work had been from the 1880's to his last days in 1959. Perhaps expecting that it might be among his last writings, *A Testament*, published two years before he died, begins with a blank page except for these few words from Alfred Lord Tennyson appearing in small print. "All may raise the flowers now for all have got the seeds."

Wright was energized by letters he received from children all over the world asking questions about his work. He would at times chuckle saying that they were trying to get him to write their term papers, but he loved the exchanges and had great faith in the youth of the world. In his *Autobiography* under the heading of "Youth," he suggests to the reader that if his writings "seem too much like lectures, just skip them because they are intended for the young..." which leads to the next two chapters.

Vernon Swaback with Frank Lloyd Wright on the set of Chicago television studio, showcasing a Broadacre City model and, to the right, at Talisin West in Arizona.

THE UNITED CHILDREN OF EARTH

"If we are to reach real peace in the world
we shall have to begin with the children."
—Mohandas Karamchand Gandhi

The Jesuit priest, Teilhard de Chardin, maintained that "the future belongs to those who are able to give the next generations reasons for hope." What if it were possible to capture and engage the youthful enthusiasm of every new generation of the world's 4th and 5th grade children in an on-going and continuously renewing study of our shared planetary home? One man, not only believes this to be possible, he has committed his life to making it happen. This quest has a long history starting more than a century ago in Paris and four decades ago by an American who expanded the original vision and has been working on it ever since.

Bryan Beaulieu, an Arizona-based, American Frenchman, has taken up the challenge of succeeding in a venture first proposed in 1900 by another Frenchman who was unable to make it all happen. Beaulieu's version is structured to be far more educational, involving a hands-on task of truly global proportions.

The Original Attempt

The first dramatic pursuit in this direction was proposed to be built as a feature of the 1900 World's Fair in Paris. More than a century ago, Elis'ee Reclus, a French geographer proposed what he called "The Great Globe." He was motivated by the desire to find a way to make a connection in the minds of children between what they could sense by way of their own daily neighborhood experiences with the greater realities of earth that are part of their world as well. His goal, never more needed than in the present, was to "convey the brotherhood of man, employing science, art and geography, all focused on peace and goodwill."

After considering all manner of approaches, Reclus and his fellow scientists decided to create a three-dimensional replica of earth, 420 feet in diameter. What Reclus and his team failed to achieve more than a century ago, was given new life, starting with an idea that was being considered at the University of Minnesota's Institute of Technology. The University reached out to Bryan Beaulieu, an alumnus they believed would be the perfect person to make it all happen. Beaulieu, volunteered to help with the condition that what was built would be something challenging enough that it could capture the imagination of both children and his fellow alumni. He proposed that they would work together and build something wonderful on campus as an engineered, high-performance event that would attract the media. The schedule allowed no time for a rehearsal, thus no room for error.

Beaulieu had just returned from Paris where he had seen the Eiffel Tower for the first time. Still not knowing exactly how to proceed, his thought was that if the engineer Gustave Eiffel could build such an incredible structure with his relatively simple 19th century tools, it should now be possible to do something quite remarkable with the benefit of 21st century engineering and technology.

The Eiffel Tower was built of plates connected with millions of rivets. As a former exhibit builder, Beaulieu had used square aluminum tubing to quickly build display structures and was impressed with Buckminster Fuller's geodesic domes as an example of elegant triangulations. He saw building a model of Earth as a way for children to learn about their planet as well as to learn about the technology of engineering. The contemplated 1:1,000,000 scale model of Earth would be 42 ft in diameter and was planned to be assembled in four hours.

Every one of the sphere's 6000 components was designed and fabricated from scratch. The result was a whole new way of mapping the planet. A child-safe connection system was invented along with a child-powered lifting crane by way of a bicycle which the children would take turns pedaling. A group of 200 volunteer alumni engineers were recruited and used to deliver panel production kits containing plastic sheets, paints, maps, fasteners, and atlases to elementary schools throughout the state of Minnesota. Hundreds of undergrads were engaged as mentors, helping the children to become "engineers for a day."

On build day 11,000 children showed up, with each one getting to put part of their planet together. They signed their panels as well as each other's hard hats then proceeded to experience the joy of building. Beaulieu said the project had cost over $100 per child but it was the best money he'd ever spent in an effort to, "inspire, especially children, to see themselves as creators and not just consumers."

After 10 more successful assemblies attended by tens of thousands of young and old, the Globe's next venues were scheduled to be set up on the West Bank by Israeli and Palestinian children. Before that could happen, the globe was destroyed by a tornado but by then it was abundantly clear that the children who participated no longer saw the world as being defined by political boundaries. There were no good or bad places and everything was connected. This was a modern day barn-raising in which all who participated felt clearly that they were not only building their shared home but their shared future.

Expanding the Mission

While that was the end of the 42 foot diameter globe, it was just the beginning of Beaulieu's belief in what the power and commitment of children could mean for the future. The only question was how to best facilitate and take advantage of what the children of the world represent and have to offer. What he believed and saw in their lives was something he didn't see in higher grades where education lead more in the direction of specialization than anything reflecting the fundamentally holistic reality of nature.

Beaulieu recalls his sophomore year in the spring of 1970, sitting in an auditorium at the University of Minnesota. He was listening to a lecture about ecology and the plans for something called "Earth Day." The lecture was being given to the engineering students who were required to take a few liberal arts courses to "round our their education." The one thing he felt certain about was that the future of earth required more than having its "Day" and whatever else it was, in terms of education, it deserved more than to be considered a "required specialty."

A quarter century later Beaulieu and his staff were engaged in moving the 42 foot diameter replica of earth to its various venues while also working on what he planned to have happen next. On April 19, 1995 he was on the mall in Washington D.C. watching thousands of kids re-erect the original five-story high 1993 University of Minnesota globe in front of the Smithsonian Castle. This 25th anniversary celebration of Earth Day was being sponsored by Lockheed Martin while a smaller globe that Beaulieu had designed for the California Science Center was being set up by kids from the Los Angeles elementary schools.

The Washington project involved thousands of local children. Some pedaled the bikes that powered the raising of the structure while others screwed 4,000 struts and hubs together and attaching the 1,620 surface panels required to create the geodesic model of Earth. Another group of

students, working in the shadow of the main globe, included more than a hundred students from the West Indies island of St. Thomas, who were in Beaulieu's words, "working on the future."

After the students had assembled their tiles they went off to explore the great museums and monuments in what they called "their" capital. This referred to the action in 1917 when in order to control the Panama Canal during WWI, St. Thomas, St. Croix, and St. John were purchased by the U.S. Many of the students returned to the Smithsonian much sooner than expected. They said the Washington monuments were nice, but they came back explaining that, "They wanted to be close to the monument they had built."

That these kids were able to participate in making their tiles of the Earth is somewhat unbelievable but their real challenge was getting to Washington D.C. Most of them had never been off their island of 50,000 residents. They held bake sales and washed cars and still came up $6000 short to pay for their plane fare. One of their teachers contributed money from his own savings to make up the difference.

Beaulieu worked closely with the Smithsonian Institution and the National Science Foundation on the Washington Project, but when he explained that the next phase of the program was to build a globe 10 times the diameter of the one sitting on the Mall they were not encouraging. The simple truth is that the representatives of the National Science Foundation thought the students would be incapable of completing such a complex project.

Beaulieu had high hopes that the publicity from the Washington project would kick start the Great Globe Project into high gear. Tragically, at that moment the death and devastation caused by Timothy McVeigh proved more newsworthy. He blew up the Oklahoma Federal building at the exact moment the children were building the globe. The Capital Mall was locked down, thus denying the project its chance to become part of history. Meanwhile on the West Coast thousands of children from around the Los Angeles area were pasting 14,600 colored paper triangles on to a 10 ft. rotating model of Earth. The California Science Center on the USC campus also wanted to celebrate the 25th anniversary of Earth Day for which Beaulieu created a smaller motorized globe. He sent 181 triangular maps out to schools around LA. Each 12 inch triangle was divided into 81 smaller triangles about an inch and a quarter on a side. The students were given instructions on how to find their part of the world. They would then look for pictures in old magazines that had the same colors that they thought best represented their area which were then cut into triangles and pasted onto the map.

The paper maps were laminated onto 20 plastic thermoformed spherical panels and attached to the 10 foot diameter framework. The resultant globe was a dazzling kaleidoscope of color that bore a clear resemblance to our planet. Hundreds of kids were filmed cutting and pasting tiny colored paper triangles to create a beautiful model of their world all made out of what would have otherwise been discarded as trash.

Beaulieu was not only inspired, as it turns out, he was just getting started. Here in brief is how he describes the background of his present quest. "We all know how quickly computerized games have co-opted the attention of young minds, too often to the exclusion of other far more worthy pursuits, including being interested and excited about life itself. The danger of this disconnect from the reality of nature is dramatized by children who say they like playing indoors because that's where all the electrical outlets are. This might seem amusing if it weren't, more realistically, terrifying.

Considering how easily the digital age has fired up and dominated the interests of children, what if that same enthusiastic spirit could be applied to something so positively enriching that their lives might be redirected to a more creative purpose. This would be far different than the time now spent playing the variety of computer games, many of which are based on conquering or destroying the enemy. And what a life – altering experience it could be if the ever–increasing reach of computational power could lead to a rich and creative understanding of the planetary home we all share, an understanding both local and global, all approached at the most engaging level of youthful enthusiasm, exploration and creativity.

The Start of the Great Globe

The original 42ft. globe's surface area was made up of painted 36 inch triangular flat panels. The St. Thomas students, along with thousands of others from the islands had made over 6,000 3D, micro tiles cut out of clear plastic sheets. This level of detail was made possible by kits that Beaulieu's staff had sent to the schools along with topographic maps, materials, and the tools needed to fabricate a model of Earth at the scale of 1/100,000. This represented a thousand-fold volumetric increase from the 42 foot diameter original, and this is the work that is currently underway.

Beaulieu's planning strategy for creating a global children's enterprise involves 100 design and fabrication studios in strategic locations all around the world. The first of these, is being operated by 4th and 5th grade children as the model for all the others to follow. This prototype for the other laboratories is located in Mesa, Arizona at the East Valley Institute of Technology where the children have full access to the latest digital technology including laser cutters, 3D color printers, and the use of NASA's 3D satellite imaging.

Each of the hundred studios are planned to produce approximately 130 tiles a day. In place of the limited experience of playing computer games, the result is that millions of children will learn the miraculous way in which their planet works all with the benefit of continuously updated technology.

In using solid modeling software to create virtual products, the students will also be exposed to the math and science that underlies the process.

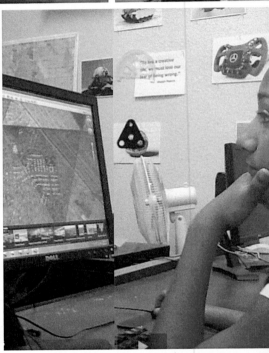

These young children, full of joy and hope, are more than observers. They are the builders of all they see. In the photo to the right, Bryan Beaulieu is introducing the process to a new crew of builders.

They will work both individually and in teams to design and create the 10,600,000 triangular, four inch tiles required to cover the rotating 420 ft diameter globe. Each student or group of students will be analyzing and computer-modeling their own 18 square mile section of the planet using data from NASA coupled with their own research. Everything about the activity is designed to get students connected with mentors in the arts and sciences as they work together to catalog the places and events that shape their individual planetary locations.

On-Going Education

In order for this to be an ongoing experience available to each new class of students, the globe is envisioned to be under continual renewal with all tiles being replaced every five to seven years. Only the diameter of the globe will remain the same. The changing patterns of earth, along with the ever-increasing observational power of technology will continue to offer insights that only time can provide. The whole quest is one of addressing the most basic and exciting elements of our human experience. The first being the relative timelessness of nature, and the second, the ever-increasing reach of our technology, commitment and the pursuit of understanding at this most holistic of all levels.

Given our use of satellite technologies along with the exponentially increasing reach of computational power, the concept has been devised to inspire and engage a spirit of global cooperation, with earth becoming a spherical board game incorporating ever-more dazzling technologies. Beaulieu's strategy is designed to have matters of global significance be enthusiastically addressed by children, more in a spirit of discovery than anything to do with fear or any other of our outmoded grown-up defenses that so limit what we are able to achieve.

Impossible Dream or Significant Reality?

Every corporation, municipality, state, and nation has experienced the uncertainties involved in carrying out major commitments. Nothing may be more risky than to outline the steps for that which is both visionary and global, but this is what is contemplated along with the status of that which already exists. The model on the preceding page represents a tangible and giant step. It is a fully activated, rotating replica of earth. The eventual 420-foot diameter globe will be located as the central feature of a surrounding, full-scale functioning community of the future. It will portray a future where stewardship along with the orchestration of shared use augments and, in some cases, replaces ownership and where the relatedness of all things replaces commodification of the pieces, and where in keeping with nature's example, nothing is ever thrown out. It is a place where exploration replaces argument and where the most needed wisdom of all is to be found in studying the one great book of nature. The most-asked questions, all important to address, relate to the Great Globe's methods of construction, its overall cost and, what about it relates to the success of humanity? All good questions, for which Beaulieu offers the following responses.

Technology

"The Eiffel Tower built in 1889 was designed with pencil on paper, without the availability of telephones or computers. One hundred percent of the 18,000 horse-delivered parts were fitted without rejects to an accuracy of .004 of an inch, the same tolerances used in today's aircraft industry. The tower was proposed as an art project and was completed in two years.

By comparison, the globe project seems almost ridiculously simple given the 21st century advantage of computer-aided design, robot fabrication, and instantaneous worldwide communication. The components of the geodesic structure are right out of the catalog of the Spanish firm, "Lanik." The gantry lifting system uses standard tower crane components. The circular observation ring consists of stock pedestrian-bridge construction, and the globe-rotating components use existing monorail drive technologies.

In 1995 the original 1993 University of Minnesota Globe was set up in front of the Washington Monument in Washington DC as part of the 20th anniversary of Earth Day. The set was sponsored by Lockheed Martin and the Smithsonian Institution. Thousands of local DC middle school students and students from the Virgin Islands helped set up the globe. Over 200,000 people attended the celebration on the Mall.

Compared to a bridge or dam The Great Globe Project is a walk in the park. A bridge structure has the same tension/compression technical issues as the globe but it also has to contend with all the environmental approvals, community buy-ins, transportation issues, government permits, and working with midair type-challenges. Working with the selected site requires dealing only with the local County building codes and Mother Nature."

Cost Comparisons

- Indian gaming resorts and casinos can cost in the range of $440 million (the equivalent cost of one globe).
- The Dallas Cowboy's new football stadium cost $1.15 billion (Almost 3 Globes)
- At one of their lowest months, video game sales were "down" to $1.9 billion (4 Globes)
- And every month kids buy 10 million pairs of Nike basketball shoes. At $80 a pair the cost of the Globe represents two weeks of sales.
- The first day sales of a recent video game totaled more than twice the cost of the Globe

Scale

The topography and coloring of the natural and man-made features to be represented on the entire 420 foot diameter globe is made up of 3D color-printed triangles measuring 4 inches on a side. If each of the required 10.6 million tiles were produced by one child, it would require only two out of every hundred children on earth to complete the task. It is likely that many more will want to become involved. With respect to how quickly children can be mobilized, consider that Facebook, which didn't even exist a decade ago, has over a billion users worldwide (665 million/day). Any child with a digital phone can become involved with his or her new global "neighborhood" being as close as the speed of light and sound.

A highly detailed 1:87 scale model of the Great Globe was constructed to verify engineering concepts and illustrate the many unique features of the project. The 5 ft globe rotates at a 33.3 degree angle within the blue observation ring where visitors can walk around the world on two levels to see Earth's 3D landscape up close. The 1/4 mile ring lowers to ground level for an unobstructed view of the planet from a distance. Assembly robots ride around the ring applying tile panels to the globes surface. A 10,000 seat amphitheater is located under the globe for concerts, plays, and lectures. A lazy river water-feature circles the amphitheater allowing visitors to float around the world. A 300 ft diameter inner platform with a 350 ft interior height is designed to be used as a planetarium or for Imax type projection.

Related Comments
At Stonehenge they used only other stones for tools. And like the ceremonial use of Stonehenge, the globe is also, in a sense, an observatory, lined up with the universe.

The Great Globe Project will become a gift to the united children of the world. It will be their enthusiasm that will cause the program to expand exponentially as something engaging, rewarding, optimistic, and of great value and fun.

We are all children of Earth. We are literally made of the Earth. When we are born we are approximately 75% water, about the same percentage as the surface of Earth that is covered by water. Other than the label 'Earthling', we are entering a time when all other cultural identity subdivisions may come to seem somewhat arbitrary. The children participating in this project will be among the first to see themselves as citizens of this most amazing of all the known planets.

Selecting the Site
Beaulieu had a dream that the globe would be sheltered in a rocky canyon so he set out to find this place of his dreams. In 1999, he sold his company and moved to Arizona knowing that the globe was going to be built somewhere in the Southwest. He had spent the prior five years looking at a diversity of other sites while still running his exhibit manufacturing and sales operation, based in Minnesota.

A structure 420 ft in diameter, enclosing almost 39 million cubic feet of space (that's two million more than the Empire State Building), needs a good foundation and remembering that the prior 42ft structure was destroyed by a tornado, he wanted to keep this much larger globe out of the wind, as well as to not dominate or visibly mar the natural environment. The search was for a site that could have year-around access, be within reasonable proximity to an international airport, and with easy connections to major highways.

Dozens of potential box canyons and craters were identified using topographic maps from the USGS along with visual surveys from chartered helicopters. Expeditions were launched in Nevada and Arizona with many of the sites being eventually eliminated due to their wilderness designations by the U.S. Bureau of Land Management.

After pursuing sites that for one reason or another were rejected, Beaulieu's team observed a dark patch in the middle of Arizona's Sonoran desert that turned out to be an extinct volcano remnant which the crater had eroded into a box canyon. The canyon walls were over 500 ft. high which would afford the desired protection. Unlike many of the sites that had been studied, this one was free of any designations as a wilderness area, national monument, or park. Thousands of saguaros grew amongst the black basalt rocks that covered the flatlands and hillsides. It turned out to be a place of uncommon landforms and great beauty.

Later when Beaulieu along with a contingent of the Tohono O'odham tribe made a pilgrimage to the site, it was determined that according to tribal history, their ancestors came to this desert over 10,000 years ago. In a cave just south of the site there are reported to be skeletons of saber tooth tigers with spear points in them. The tribe did not have a written language until the 1930s. History was recorded on a Calendar Stick used to mark important events.

The Tohono O'odham's tribal icon is the "Man in the Maze" symbol. This seven circuit labyrinth dates back to ancient Crete. Walking the labyrinth represents life's journey. The switchbacks sometimes bring you towards your dreams, sometimes away from them. When you reach the middle of the labyrinth you have reached your goal, the end of this life as we know it.

This beautiful and rare site, appears to have been prepared by nature, both to host and shelter the great globe as a perfect setting for the surrounding village. It will be a place to celebrate the new world, all lovingly created by the children who will be the new world's citizen leaders of the first, understanding – based, global community.

Beaulieu's Anticipation of Doubters

"To practical people I must look like Don Quixote, pursuing the impossible dream. But those impossible dreams are what we tell young children to strive for. 'You can be anything you want in life. Follow you dreams.' As they get older, however, we want them to get practical and prepare to get a good paying job. They will have to wait for retirement to find their bliss."

"In the business world a CEO is supposed to be visionary but a person with visions is regarded as mentally ill. Politics is about doing practical things for the community but president Kennedy proposed one of the most impractical projects; putting a man on the moon. It was not his first choice for some grand project but he felt he needed something to bolster his position after the Bay of Pigs fiasco."

"The Apollo program cost 20% more than the entire Interstate Highway System, and was criticized at the time by the head of NASA as the wrong project to pursue, but we still refer to it today as a shining example of what is possible with our all-out commitment."

"In his memorable speech in 1962, at Rice University in Texas, Kennedy said, 'we choose to go the moon not because it is easy but because it is hard.' I think of that a lot when working on the globe."

"We travel the world in search of the impractical. What good is the Great Pyramid, the Eiffel Tower, Stonehenge, or Notre Dame? They were all impractical dreams that made it into reality and continue to inspire each new generation."

Who will own the Great Globe?

As the project begins to emerge from the privacy of its initial laboratory, it is attracting a great deal of interest, including suggestions for other locations both in the U.S. and elsewhere around the world. The already described site is on the Nation of the Tohono O'odham, whose tribal council has jurisdiction over the land.

As for the nuances of "ownership," a good precedent to consider might be something like the United Nations Headquarters in New York City. The site, which once housed a former slaughterhouse, was purchased for the UN by John D. Rockefeller Jr. for 8.5 million dollars. The buildings were designed jointly by Le Corbusier and Oscar Niemeyer. It is technically not part of the United States but extraterritorial. The UN gets police and fire protection from the city and agrees to most local, state, and federal laws. Given this precedent, the site for the Great Globe could be owned in spirit by the United Children of Earth. It could be a neutral territory where the world's children are able to have a common experience in the presence of the massive and artful monument to community, one that they have created.

When asked to answer what his chances are for making this happen Beaulieu responds with a question. He asks if we know what the best-selling book is of all time, other than books, like the Bible, that have an organized mandate behind their sales. When those asked acknowledge that they don't have a clue Beaulieu seems pleased to inform them that the honor belongs to *Don Quijote,* first published in 1605.

All that can be said in answer to many other questions is that Beaulieu is a 21st century Don Quijote who has a degree in engineering and has run a thousand person company. The Great Globe project is his all-consuming passion for which he feels successful every time he helps another child think of his or her home as being that of planet earth. Perhaps we could add to this George Bernard Shaw's insistence that "All progress depends on the unreasonable man."

Welcome to the UCE

Bucky Fuller set the stage for the *United Children of Earth* when he proclaimed that "on spaceship earth, there are no passengers, only crew." Bryan Beaulieu is giving the youngest members of the crew the tools to learn and share more about their whole earth neighbors than that which has been compiled by all the prior generations combined.

These young "Earth Surveyors", are given all the tools they need to find out about things that are contained or have happened in their respective study areas. The children enter what they learn into the Great Globe Data Base, saved in Microsoft's Skydrive internet cloud storage. Each student is allocated 25 gigabytes of information space which is equivalent to about 12,500 full length books. They are also able to record audio and video amounting to more than 6,000 high-resolution pictures.

This information can be accessed by anyone on the Internet just by entering the Tile Number. The data is not vetted but it is linked with the Earth Surveyor's I.D. number, allowing it to be challenged on the Great Globe website. For example if one of the "Earth Surveyors" report that there are camels living in Phoenix, Arizona, near Camelback Mountain, as indicated on tile D761615, anyone questioning this can email Earth Surveyor #567-678-456 to ask for documentation. The response would likely be that there are 10 camels at the Phoenix Zoo. At every five to seven year cycle the data for each site is both altered and refined as the next group of children produce the new generation of tiles. As the technology is expanded and refined, it becomes the ever-increasing best of two worlds, one involving genuine hands-on exploration and the other being as enticing as the latest video game. The difference is that this one represents an educational significance of global proportions.

Individual groups of students from all over the world will assemble the 10.5 million 3D tiles and mounting structures required to cover the 420 feet model of Earth. Each 1:100,000 scale, triangular areas will be researched and recorded by the students for the Great Globe data base. Mentors help the students build the precision tile assemblies and guide them on their investigations for their parts of the planet.

The children's 40-story replica of the planet earth is shown surrounded by a 21st c
tury global village epitomizing the always-welcome nature of a living city for wh
there are no divisions between function and beauty and where work and life are o

SURROUNDED BY
MIRACLES

"The task of genius, and humanity is nothing if not genius,
is to keep the miracle alive, to live always in the miracle, to
make the miracle more and more miraculous,
to swear allegiance to nothing, but to live only miraculously,
think only miraculously, die miraculously."
–Henry Miller

W e live in a multiplicity of dualities, including that which we call heaven and hell, good and evil, community and war, all played out in two worlds, the one in which we monetize in order to buy and sell and the other in which we love, nurture, and create.

We marvel as technological devices that were once huge and limited in their computational power become ever smaller and ever more effective, forgetting that nature is one great global communication system, requiring no external devices at all.

And while we quite rightly recognize technological triumphs that have the power for good, it is only by way of these accomplishments that we are now able to poison and destroy the very life source that we didn't create and we can't live without. This destroy or create duality is our daily and confusing reality, one most delightfully expressed by William H. White. "Sometimes when I get up in the morning I can't decide whether I want to savor the world or to save the world." He went on to say, "It makes it real hard the plan one's day." That sentiment, for all but the most limited or self-absorbed individuals, will become increasingly true for all of us as citizens of the world.

Inventing Our Tomorrows

Not everyone can be expected to look much beyond the obvious demands of the present. While there will always be differing views as to whether hard times or good times are best for conceptualizing anything that isn't already close at hand, history is clear on this point. For those who provide the leadership upon which all else depends, the right time for an idea to be launched, as Frank Lloyd Wright insisted, "is just as soon as someone has it."

A good start for all of us would be to agree on two quite reasonable observations. Everything other than the creation which preceded us that we call "nature," is a human invention, including the invention of language and everything we have used it to explore, shape and establish into what we refer to as "reality."

If we are willing to agree that everything beyond that which preceded our human existence, is a matter of our own creativity or invention, a good next step would be to evaluate what we might consider to be humanity's most enduring accomplishments. While we might tend to shrug this off as an impossible task, one man has written a 668 page compendium under the title, *Human Accomplishment: The Pursuit of Excellence in the Arts and Sciences, 800 B.C. to 1950*. Written by the distinguished researcher and author, Charles Murray, this exhaustive work is organized into four parts. Part one, addresses, "A sense of Accomplishment. This is followed by "Identifying the People and Events that Matter," "Patterns and Trajectories," and, "The Origin and Decline of Accomplishments."

I introduce this study, not to debate who did or did not make the list, but only to reinforce that the state of the world is nothing more than a consolidated record of what we all think, believe, and achieve. Being armed, as we are with this awesome power to not only think and believe but also to honor, invent, and create, quite clearly calls upon all of us to give the future the finest we each have to offer.

The idea of "giving our best" starts with some level of definitional understanding and agreement. For example, peace is the absence of war. Community is the opposite of war. Peace is something that can be felt in one's heart. It is to feel a sense of well-being with yourself, with others, and with circumstances from the local to the global. Community differs from peace in that it consists of our most challenging and dynamic interactions. A sense of community can be like the spirit of a well-played game, including winners and losers, both bound by the same rules and all energized by the unknown outcome resulting from the cooperative and competitive actions on the field of play.

Like all things cooperative and competitive, our shared behaviors can range from the brute force of the physical to the complexities of the artful, and from argumentative matters of individual "taste" to the disciplined performance of a great symphony. Community requires no less strategic planning, allegiance, innovation, and investment than the attack and defenses of war, it just starts with a different motivation, all designed for a far different outcome. Failure with respect to the demands of community will tend to incite mobilization in the direction of conflict. All it takes to understand that we are more easily obsessed with conflict than community is to compare the range and number of movies that dramatize the obviousness of brutality over the nuances of compassion. Considering the media's mandate that, "if it bleeds, it leads," our daily diet of violence, especially that which is dramatized on the TV newscasts with musical fanfares and whirling graphics, is not likely to give way to discussing the miraculous nature of photosynthesis, notwithstanding that without it there could be neither "news" nor life.

Yet, as we have seen from the exhaustive studies of others, despite the incessant delivery of mind-numbing conflict, humanity is, however slowly, moving in the direction of non-violence. War is a triumph of fear over reason. On the side of fear, we are beginning to realize that the strategic deployment of our latest technology threatens both our own immediate interests as well as the long-term prospects for everything to follow.

With respect for how we plan for the future, the new frontier of community has a focus that goes well beyond both the city forms produced by the Industrial Revolution and the disbursed patterns of development that followed WWII. This new direction will not be driven by style or urban form as much as it will by a search for the beauty and relationships that both inspire our highest commitments while responding to our desire for life-long purpose and fulfillment.

As previously noted, Winton Churchill said we Americans could always be counted to do exactly the right thing just as soon we explored and discounted all other options. What if we could phrase a more global version, one influenced by everything we've all learned since the time of Churchill. For example, considering that the world's leaders have tried high-level conferences, treaties, blockades, and spying along with the evermore powerful and high tech measures to destroy and defend, might it be time to consider something short and clear like the following:

> All parties have agreed that shaping a new approach to a sustainable way of life by programming and design is preferable to the old way of working things out by way of death and destruction. Having now spent centuries trying to reap the rewards of war, the pursuit of community has now risen to a more mutually beneficial way for the future. While the process has been glacially slow, it appears that our biological wiring that seemed to favor the lose/lose behaviors of kill or be killed has little-by-little been overtaken by the emergence of cultural/technological behaviors that favor live and let live.

For each of the last 40 years *Freedom House* has analyzed, evaluated and provided an account of the number and state of democratic institutions using metrics like the level of civil liberties and freedom of the press, along with elections utilizing proper ballot security and tabulation. In 1973, as part of their "Freedom in the World" analysis, they listed 15 qualifying countries. From year to year this number either remained the same or increased. By 2013 their original count of 151 "Free Countries" bad grown to 195. [1]

Robert Wright's Non-Zero: The Logic of Human Destiny, brings a critically needed perspective to current events in a way that enables us to better understand their direction. And the directions he portrays are among the most positive ways to unite everything we know about the past with everything we hope for the future. Here in just two sentences is a core summary of his 435 page analysis: "As history progresses, human beings find themselves playing non-zero-sum games with more and more other human beings. Interdependence expands, and social complexity grows in scope and depth." [2] In other words, contrary to what can be observed from any one moment in time, the long-range human trajectory of cooperative behavior is positive. In the words of Frank Lloyd Wright "as long as we are still in the process of becoming, we are still safe."

More than Physical Proximity

Many individuals live on side-by-side lots in suburbia, or in high-rise apartments, without having the slightest interaction with those living a few feet, or in the case of the apartment dweller, a few inches away from their neighbors. We do a disservice to the deeper understanding of community to think of it as being limited to physical proximity. Consider, for example, the works of Bach, Michelangelo, Einstein, Frederick Law Olmsted, and Frank Lloyd Wright. They represent individuals who contributed to the culture of community each by way of their respective pursuits of sound, sculpture, science, places, spaces, and structures, all individually produced and each in their own way, extraordinary works of art.

To fully understand the works of these five individuals is to get closer to the idea of community in its deepest sense. The community of Bach, consists of the commitment of performers and audiences who play and hear what Bach composed in solitude. The community of Michelangelo is symbolized by those who have cried in the presence of his "David" because they felt connected to something beyond the reach of words. Most people would have no way to understand the complexity of Einstein's special and general relativity, but the poetry and clarity of his more spiritual observations have enriched our sense of wonder. Individuals who walk and play in the beauty of Olmsted's Central Park, as well as those who live, work or visit Frank Lloyd Wright's creations, experience something that can't be explained by a description of their respective features, materials, colors or any other physical measures. The work of these five individuals epitomize essential components of community, not by their physical proximity or participation in the group, but by way of their widely-shared creations of inspiring designs that enrich us all.

Those who dream of a better world must make sense to those who only know how to fear. Our two worlds view of the future is occurring between the fear of chaos and the fear of order. Like all dualities, the embrace between chaos and order is a source of great energy. The trajectory of our cultural evolution is toward a unity of shared purpose. The kind of unity which exists to the advantage of some very special places is moving toward existing in all places, both local and global. If chaos overtakes order, there will be no human future. If order overtakes chaos, there will be no human freedom. And although this behavioral duality may seem to make humanity at war with itself, this is our best attempt to stay on nature's evolutionary path. It is what Dee Hock, a most remarkable visionary, called the "birth of the Chaordic age", defining "Chaordic" as any self-organizing, self-governing, nonlinear, complex organism, organization, community or system, whether physical, biological or social, the behavior of which harmoniously blends the characteristics of both chaos and order."[3] As the founder and CEO Emeritus of VISA, Dee Hock was no stranger to the ways and means of the free market. At the same time his judgments concerning anything to do with human values requires a far different and deeper sense of commitment as expressed in his definition of community.

"The essence of community, its very heart and soul, is the non-monetary exchange of value; things we do and share because we care for others, and for the good of the place. Community is composed largely of that which we don't attempt to measure, for which we keep no record and ask no recompense. Most are things we cannot measure no matter how hard we try. Since they can't be measured, they can't be denominated in dollars, or barrels of oil, or bushels of corn – such things as respect, tolerance, love, trust, beauty – the supply of which is unbounded and unlimited. The non-monetary exchange of value does not arise solely from altruistic motives. It arises from deep, intuitive, often subconscious understanding that self-interest is inseparably connected with community interest; that individual good is inseparable from the good of the whole; that in some way, often beyond our understanding, all things are, at one and the same time, independent, interdependent, and intradependent.

Without an abundance of non-material values and an equal abundance of non-monetary exchange of material value, no true community ever existed or ever will. Community is not about profit. It is about benefit. We confuse them at our peril. When we attempt to monetize all value, we methodically disconnect people and destroy community.

The non-monetary exchange of value is the most effective, constructive system ever devised. Evolution and nature have been perfecting it for thousands of millennia. It requires no currency, contracts, government, laws, courts, police, economists, lawyers, and accountants. It does not require anointed or certified experts at all. It requires only ordinary, caring people." [4]

As already observed, the most powerful, exciting and sustainable system, that of nature itself, involves a seamless duality between cooperation and competition. The power and beauty of such a system cannot be understood by analyzing its constituent parts. It only exists in its wholeness. Our evolutionary path is in that direction. Will we get there, and with much evidence to suggest that we will, how much continued loss and carnage must we confront along the way? Everyone who has ever marketed a product, lobbied on behalf of a law, argued in support of a scientific theory or crusaded on behalf of their religious beliefs has one thing in common. Einstein said it best. "Setting an example is not only the best way to lead, it is the only way."

One of Buckminster Fuller's, most hopeful statements starts by acknowledging humanity's near incurable tendency to fear. He then proceeds to present humanity's near inevitable trajectory for success. "There are very few men today who are disciplined to comprehend the totally integrating significance of the 99 percent invisible activity which is coalescing to reshape our future. There are no warnings being given the society regarding the great changes ahead. There is only the ominous general apprehension that man may be about to annihilate himself. To the few who are disciplined to deal with the invisibly integrating trends it is increasingly readable that man is about to become almost 100 percent successful as an occupant of the universe." [5]

Being both inspired and emboldened by Fuller's always universal insights, consider these challenging words from Thom Hartmann who connects the art of community to our most personal commitments concerning what we are both individually and collectively becoming.

126

"The work of the community serves as a galvanizing point, a shared effort that is, in the simple act of doing it, a living out of the vision...There are parallels to this in individual life as well. When a person doesn't feel a sense of mission or purpose in their work, their life often slides, rudderless, toward a dull cardboard – like existence... People who have a sense of mission about their work are happier, more motivated, more productive, and more likely to remain healthy, both physically, emotionally, psychologically, and spiritually."[6]

This powerful recognition of the essential need and blessings of community has been experienced by most individuals and groups at special moments with special people. The goal is to extend this feeling to the world of everyday living. This is nothing more or less than giving our individual best to the artful wholeness of life itself, including the global art of community.

Joseph S. Nye Jr. is University Distinguished Service Professor at Harvard University, who in December 2010 offered these observations in the direction of a greater need for cooperation between nations. "The problem of American power in the twenty-first century, is not one of decline but what to do in light of the realization that even the most powerful country cannot achieve the outcomes it wants without the help of others. An increasing number of challenges will require a deeper understanding of power, how it is changing, and how to construct "smart power" strategies that combine hard-and-soft-power resources in the information age. The country's capacity to maintain alliances and create networks will be an important dimension of its hard and soft power."[7]

If "hard" is meant to convey the threat or use of power, soft power is ultimately a nation's ability to make less obvious demands on others. The recognition here is that given that hard power speaks to that which can be demanded, and if necessary upheld by exercising a superior position for which the ultimate expression is war, soft power calls upon the art of mutually beneficial relationships. A safe assumption for the 21st century that favors soft power over intimidation, is that the once clear strength of having a superior position by location and technology has been replaced with a world connected, both at its worst and its best, at the speed of light and sound.

The success of military might or other forms of national dominance is simply incompatible with our new global relationships. Joseph Campbell reminds us that "We need myths that will identify the individual not with his local group but with the planet. When you see the Earth from the moon you don't see any divisions of nations or states." [48] Campbell sees this as the symbol for all that is yet to be.

Behavioral or social agreements evolve at a far slower rate than technological inventions as expressed in the phrase, "you can't change human nature." This familiar rant is not only dangerously outmoded, it simply isn't true. If you've ever experienced or watched others crying their eyes out while listening to a great work of art like Mozart's *Ave Verum* or witnessed teary-eyed people gathered around Michelangelo's David, you are experiencing the behavioral-influencing power of design.

Harold Bloom's best-selling volume on Shakespeare is subtitled, *The Invention of the Human*. Consistent with the examples of Mozart, Michelangelo and Shakespeare, the creative reach of design is that which has the power to bypass the limitations of our grown-up defenses that so easily keep us in a state of turmoil and loss. A related example of this is addressed in Riane Eisler's The Chalice and the Blade which shines an uncommon light on the backward steps that we so easily mistake for exciting insights into the future.

> "Science fiction writers' visions of the future are filled with incredible technological inventions. But by in large, their's is a world singularly bereft of new social inventions. In fact, more often than not, what they envision takes us backward while seeming to

go forward in time. Be it in Frank Herbert's Dune or George Lucas's *Star Wars*, what we frequently find is actually the social organization of feudal emperors and medieval overlords transposed to a world of intergalactic high-tech wars." [8]

The kind of masculine energy which exists in both male of female that so easily focuses on argument and on "conquering," is giving way to a far more complex understanding of relationships and accommodations. It is as great a mistake to think of being able to conquer each other as it is to think of being able conquer nature. The more we humans grow in number, consumption per capita, and in technological power, the more we have to search for ways to live that are as "orchestrated" as a great symphony. This means recognizing not only our differences but also our commitments to the overall success of the group. Referring again to Bucky Fuller's reminder that, "On spaceship earth, there are no passengers, only crew," we are waking up to the reality that these relationships are all matters of design.

Wherever designing for life is the goal, the real and ultimate competition is with ourselves. But without the possibility for engaging with others, life is bereft of meaning. In the words of Albert Einstein. "The individual, if left alone from birth, would remain primitive and beastlike in his thoughts and feelings to a degree that we can hardly conceive. The individual is what he is, not so much in virtue of this individuality, but rather as a member of a great human community, which directs his material and spiritual existence from the cradle to the grave."

That which we've shaped that now shapes us, including religion, technology, economics, politics and law is either creatively useful or dreadfully destructive, all as related to the overall system in which they serve as component parts. For the world of design, this requires addressing, not only relationships between individuals and nations but of critical importance, to that of our shared partnering with the ecosystem services of earth. Everything anyone has ever committed to action, good or bad, is a kind of design. A large wall-mounted banner that has long hung in a conference room shared by Swaback Partners and the Two Worlds Community Foundation states, *We are moving from the world of design to the design of the world.* That "we" goes well beyond any one group to include all of us as citizens of earth.

Everyone from musicians and dancers to scholars and athletes, know that high performance requires never-ending discipline and practice. In his 89th year, Frank Lloyd Wright said, "One of the things I like most about myself is that I can still learn something." In his nineties, the great cellist Pablo Casals was asked why he continued to practice. His simple answer was, "I think I am getting better."

We are living at the center of urgent joy – urgent because we now know that to fail would be catastrophic, and joyful, because we are beginning to understand that to succeed will require a level of beneficial coexistence with nature and each other, far beyond what we've ever believed to be possible. We are kept alive and alert by our thoughts and commitments which are in themselves, a kind of design. In the *Ascent of Man*, Jacob Bronowski wrote, "We have to understand that the world can only be grasped by action, not by contemplation...the most powerful drive in the ascent of man is his pleasure in his own skill. He loves to do what he does well, and having done it well, he loves to do it better." The greatest art of all, the one that ultimately matters most, because it is necessary to give meaning to the rest, is the art of community, which is to say - from the local to the global - the creative art of relationships.

THE CREATIVE
COMMUNITY

"The future belongs to those who are able to give the next

generations reasons for hope."

--Teilhard de Chardin

I've come to see the wealth of life-enriching experiences during my Taliesin years as a time when seeds were being planted for later harvest. One such flowering was the 2003 publication of *The Creative Community: Designing for Life* which overlapped with meeting a woman who had just opened a K-12 school, for which I had been told she had no background and less funding to keep it alive.

In hindsight what she clearly possessed was an ability to interest others in her passionate commitment to revolutionize the methods of education for those who needed it the most. My contact with her started when the word went out that attracted a variety of volunteers to help her clean up a a pretty awful looking property that she had leased to house her newly named *StarShine Academy*. Hearing of this a member of my firm urged that I consider designing and executing a large-scale mural that would go somewhere on the otherwise drab walls. This didn't seem very inspiring and all I could think of was that the individual doing the urging had no idea as to what that would involve. I agreed to meet this school-founding lady, assuming that was as far as my involvement would go.

To make matters even less appealing, the founder of this school seemed pleased as to how she had selected her property. Having been influenced by the rant of our developer clients saying that the three most important decisions for their projects were, "location, location, and location," it was somewhat worrisome to hear that she had selected her location because it had the city's "highest crime rate, its highest rate of school drop-outs, and its highest incidence of teen pregnancies."

Nonetheless, the requested meeting occurred. As I had feared there was absolutely nothing inspiring about either the location or the structures. What I didn't know to expect was that Trish, the woman at the heart of it all was both striking in her appearance and immediately engaging in what she had to say. We met in a tiny retrofitted office which contained her desk, a couch and two guest chairs, all of which left very little room to place one's feet. That which gave a ray of hope was the wall-to-wall, floor-to-ceiling collage of inspiring quotations intermixed with photos of seemingly happy, vibrant children.

Two hours of conversation passed before I realized that we had not yet even mentioned the mural, which was my sole reason for being there. It really didn't matter because by then we were all crying our eyes out over whatever magic our beautiful host had been spinning. To make a long story short, not only was the mural designed and executed as an integral feature of the campus, I have served as a member of StarShine Adcademy's board ever since. I tried on two occasions to resign, only to be told by Trish that resignation wasn't an option, and furthermore, she and I would be tied together for the rest of our lives.

Because she works in the proverbial "wondrous ways", there were times that I simply could not connect the dots between her sense of cause and effect. Yet she always seems to attract whatever is needed but not a minute before it would be too late. This included everything from staffing to funding and in our tenth year, even the need to find a new location, without which we would have no school.

This all occurred during April of 2011 when we were unceremoniously informed by the agent for the property, which Trish had lovingly retrofitted and maintained, that the school would have to vacate before the end of the year. Because this left precious little time to find a new home, coupled with the severely limited funding available to make the move, it seemed to some that this might be the end of a heroic journey, but those who felt this way certainly didn't include Trish.

Special challenges inspire special people. Frank Lloyd Wright once said, "All I know about money is that I need to spend it so that I can get some more." With respect to looking for property, Wright would advise his early clients, especially those who were more adventurous than wealthy, to "find something that others either didn't want or wouldn't know what to do with it." The end of 2011 and the first part of 2012 brought a series of what at first seemed to be good prospects, which all too quickly became disappointments. I thought often about Wright 's lifetime of uncommon setbacks followed by uncommon triumphs. At such times, he would say, "As long you're still in the process of becoming, you're still safe." And when overcoming all manner of problems, he would say, "Well boys, we've done it again. We've snatched victory from the jaws of defeat."

That which I want to convey most has little to do with the details of the agonizing machinations that Trish and others faced in order to save StarShine, but before I do, there is one more story to tell along the way. In 2003, Trish applied for a grant designed to fund the coaching of StarShine's students toward entrepreneurship. After a few weeks she received a call from the person who was charged with reviewing her application. The caller's bias was immediately evident. "Isn't your school located in a marginal area of the city and aren't your students what we would call kids at risk?" Trish found little to counter the implication of the officials questions, but then came the killer. "Instead of applying for a grant related to entrepreneurship wouldn't it be more appropriate to apply for one focused on machine shop work or possibly something to do with auto mechanics?"

A View From the Present

As a way to symbolize the power of an idea, no matter how impossible it may seem to others, fast forward to the morning of January 16, 2014. The setting is that of StarShine's now very own, just completed, four and a half acre campus consisting of a series of eight renovated buildings which together with two major new structures, provide the physical and spiritual environment for StarShine Adacemy's Creative Community and EcoVillage.

On this mid-January morning, well- dressed individuals representing all ages and all walks of life gathered to help celebrate StarShine's "12th Annual 100th Monkey Breakfast", named after the inspiring story about social change by Ken Keyes, Jr.

The school's bright young children were everywhere evident, first graciously greeting the arriving guests, later helping to clear the breakfast tables and, in between, starring in a choreographed dance performance which brought the cheering audience to its feet. Other elements of the program included, a guitar trio led by Steve McCarty, formerly of the Steve Miller Band and now Trish's husband, a hilarious three-person skit that engaged the entire audience, and a violin and cello duet of the highest level of performance representing the training at both Harvard and the Juilliard School of Music.

As for stretching the minds of all in attendance, Melani Walton gave the morning's featured presentation providing insights into cutting edge discoveries with respect to the workings of the human brain with its exciting potential for what it means for the creative majesty of life. To experience this presentation was to be both informed and inspired. At the conclusion of the program, the guests were invited to visit StarShine Academy's Innovation Center where tomorrow's leaders are having their concepts of the possible expanded beyond our easy imaginations. Expressed in a variety of ways, those who attended the program related that something very special had been experienced.

Remembering the well-meaning advisor who inferred to Trish that entrepreneurial training would be wasted on StarShine's students, it gives me great pleasure to note that during that same year, four of StarShine's students formed their own company. As for StarShine being blessed with the interest of very special people, the enthusiastic members of the January 16, 2014 audience included philosophic chieftains of commerce as well as leaders in the fields of neurology, homeopathic medicine, scientists, financiers, educators, musicians of all kinds and a wide variety of others that Frank Lloyd Wright revered as "our typical best citizens". Last but not least the breakfast was prepared by the head chef and staff of the Ritz Carlton, just as it had been for each and every one of StarShine's first eleven 100th Monkey celebrations.

Having laid the groundwork for expansion, this miracle-working Trish McCarty is just getting started. StarShine is accredited by North Central and the AdvancEd Commission on Trans-Regional Accreditation. With respect to her goal of establishing 1000 StarShine schools all over the world, she has had teacher training relationships with Universities in China, Liberia, Mexico, Sudan, India, London, Oxford, Dublin and Cork, Ireland. She has also conducted a series of special sessions, including those at Windsor Castle. On a more personal note, with respect to *The Creative Community: Designing for Life*, I wrote the book, but Trish McCarty is creating the communities. The eight by eighteen foot "Garden of the Stars" mural which the students helped to create is shown below.

Clockwise: The young students walking across their new campus behind a sculptural representation of the school's logo, and shown dressed for the job and ready to work with the head chef and staff of the Ritz Carlton. Trish McCarty with Gladys T. McGarey, the celebrated founder of holistic healing. Above, Melani Walton delivering a compellingly illustrated presentation concerning the latest and exciting insights into the workings of the brain.

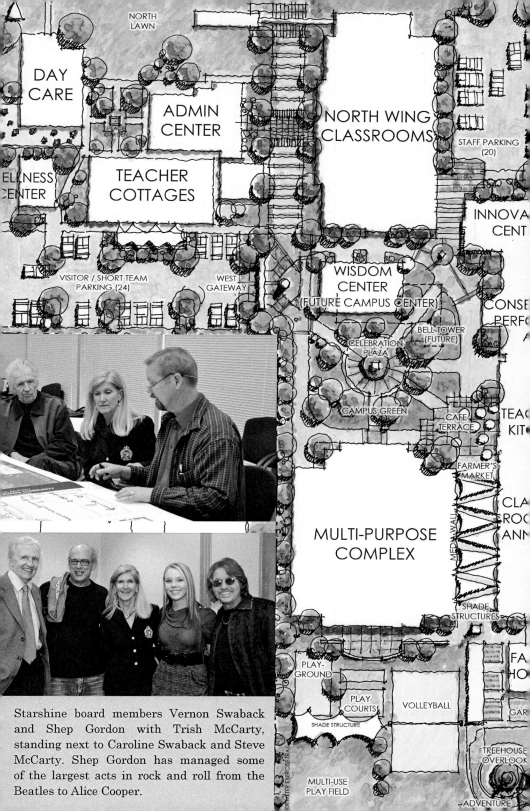

DAY CARE

NORTH LAWN

ADMIN CENTER

NORTH WING CLASSROOMS

STAFF PARKING (20)

WELLNESS CENTER

TEACHER COTTAGES

PEACE GARDEN

INNOVA CENT

VISITOR / SHORT TEAM PARKING (24)

WEST GATEWAY

WISDOM CENTER
(FUTURE CAMPUS CENTER)

CONSE PERFO A

CELEBRATION PLAZA

BELL TOWER (FUTURE)

CAMPUS GREEN

CAFE TERRACE

TEA KIT

FARMER'S MARKET

CLA ROO ANN

MEDIA WALL

MULTI-PURPOSE COMPLEX

SHADE STRUCTURES

FA HO

PLAY-GROUND

PLAY COURTS

SHADE STRUCTURE

VOLLEYBALL

GAR

PERIMETER EXERCISE TRAIL

MULTI-USE PLAY FIELD

TREEHOUSE OVERLOOK

ADVENTURE

Starshine board members Vernon Swaback and Shep Gordon with Trish McCarty, standing next to Caroline Swaback and Steve McCarty. Shep Gordon has managed some of the largest acts in rock and roll from the Beatles to Alice Cooper.

FRANK LLOYD WRIGHT CENTER FOR THE FUTURE

"To whom much is given, much will be required."

–Luke 12:48

With respect to the work and legacy of Frank Lloyd Wright, what is it that we've been given? Why has he long been called the world's greatest architect and now our first green and ecological architect? Where did this all start? How did he become who he was? His own answer to the same questions always began with, "We all get it from somewhere." He would then go on to talk about how he loved, collected, studied, and wrote about what he learned from the Japanese artists who created the wood block prints. Among his favorite artists were Hokusai, Hiroshige and Utamaro. What he saw and what inspired him most about this work was its self-conscious simplicity in which nature, people, and structures, are all beautifully presented by way of flat plane abstractions. Wright would talk about how, by way of this technique, the artist had "eliminated the insignificant", a phrase he would often use to describe as one of the objectives of his own approach to architecture.

Another, always mentioned and revered influence, was his employer and mentor, the great Louis Sullivan, whom he referred to as the father of the tall building. Not just tall in the sense of physical measures but in the spirit of what it meant for a building to reach up to the sky. Whenever Wright referred to Louis Sullivan it was always accompanied with the term "Lieber Meister".

138

The third and most abiding influence was that provided by his mother. In addition to having hung architectural prints of the world's great buildings around his crib waiting for him to be born, she introduced her young son to "Froebels Gifts". Friedrich Froebel (1782-1852) was a German educator who is credited with nurturing the idea of the "Kindergarten", which is German for, "child in the garden," as in our "kindergarden".

Wright would seem like a child, when telling about these "gifts". Writing in his 1943 Autobiography he described them as, "strips of colored paper, glazed and matte, remarkably soft brilliant colors. Now came the geometric by-play of those charming checkered color combinations! The structural figures to be made with peas and small straight sticks: slender constructions, the joinings accented by the little green-pea globes. The smooth shapely maple blocks with which to build, the sense of which never afterward leaves the fingers: *form* becoming *feeling*. The box had a mast to set up on it, on which to hang the maple cubes and spheres and triangles, revolving them to discover subordinate forms."

Even in his last years this artist-architect-crusader never stopped referring to his earliest experiences with "Froebel's gifts". This should certainly strengthen our interest in what such artistic influences can have on our youth.

Despite living and working in remote locations, Wright somehow found ways to interest much of the world in what he had to say. While other architects were, and still are, focused on style and the cleverness of form, his work and message was all about learning from, and partnering with nature. Designed with that objective in mind, he shaped and shared his own way of life as a living example of what that meant. So much so that his own live/work estates at Taliesin and Taliesin West are National Landmarks that celebrate his past while offering inspiration for today and tomorrow for all who come from all over the world to tour and learn from his example.

Wright demonstrated how the reach of design has the power to go well beyond stylistic appearance to serve as something more significantly inseparable from the vitality of life. He lived his philosophy by creating a community where the notion of retirement had no meaning, where the pursuit of living life in tune with nature was far more important than ownership, and where education, culture, and creativity were all inseparable features of living fully at all ages and stages.

To say that he practiced what he preached would be an understatement. The Taliesin way of life was steeped in the blessing of nature, affording every opportunity for creating and living in an atmosphere of both natural and man-made beauty. In the traditional sense of accounting he owned nothing. Everything he had designed, built and once owned, was put in trust for the benefit of the future, including all of us.

The View from Today

The tours of both Taliesin and Taliesin West continue in the present as they did during Frank Lloyd Wright's time. What is different today is the degree to which both venues now cater to the much larger groups of the general public, along with rather elaborate gift shops that offer an ever-increasing array of books. Also for sale are a variety of large and small objects, including china, clothing, furnishings, and DVD's, all bearing some semblance of Wright's easy to recognize geometric patterns and colors.

The visitors who were accommodated during Wright's lifetime, who may have felt that they were somewhat of an interruption to the daily activities are now central to the lifeblood of the organization. The tours are offered in a wide variety of lengths and access, all conducted by trained docents. Visitors seem well pleased with the tours, all embellished with wonderful stories about Frank Lloyd Wright including the kind that seem to well up around famous personalities, quite apart from whether or not what is being related ever happened. I've come to accept that on a less than scholarly level, perhaps this tendency to add a bit of fantasy to the historic record is not all that harmful. In a rather amusing example of this, I once witnessed Wright being told an oft-repeated story concerning one of his leaky roofs. He listened while smiling without objection. Upon hearing about how this supposedly accurate account turned out, he laughed with the rest of us then said, "That's another one of those stories. It never happened, but it's a good one – keep it going."

Expanding the Vision

As part of the planning for the 75th anniversary of Taliesin West, a major exhibition of his work was scheduled to occur at the Phoenix Art Museum. I was honored to be asked to give the keynote address at a benefit reception as part of the exhibition which was held at the museum on February 16, 2012. As we entered the Museum's beautiful Whiteman Hall, the mood was set by the sounds of Beethoven's, Emperor Concerto, one of Wright's favorites. After giving an illustrated account of Wright's inspiring legacy, I focused on the subject of his unfinished work.

I began with a question. Given the extraordinary breadth of his philosophic understanding as well as his having received every major global honor and award that could be accorded an architect, what was the one pursuit that eluded him during his long life? What was the one challenge to which he dedicated four of his books including, The Disappearing City written in 1932; *When Democracy Builds*, 1945; *The Living City*, 1958; and *The Industrial Revolution Runs Away* published posthumously in 1969?

These four books extending over a period of nearly four decades go well beyond the design of any one type of structure. They represent Frank Lloyd Wright's testimony to the orchestration of what he called Broadacre City. So misunderstood was this critical focus of his work that even some of his most ardent admirers still think that this was the one area where the great architect lost his way. While these detractors admit that Wright was profoundly accurate in what he prophesied, some believe it to be nothing more than a regrettably accurate vision for what we decry today as urban sprawl.

More than seven decades after Wright named his 1932 publication *"The Disappearing City"* –Richard Ingersoll wrote a book about the urban environment in which he observed, "Almost without notice the city has disappeared." He went on to write, "Although large populations continue to work in places with names like Rome, Paris, New York, or Beijing, the majority of the inhabitants live outside the center city."

Sprawl is one of those words that everyone uses but no one has ever felt the need to define. Here in just four words, I offer the only definition that makes any sense. "Sprawl is artless development", the very opposite of what Wright called "Broadacre City." If sprawl were translated into musical terms it would be like repeating the same note over and over again. It would drive us all insane. Not so long ago I was driving a friend to her home. Once inside her subdivision I asked, "Do I turn here?" No. "Do I turn here?" No. After several such questions, my passenger offered this assistance, "Our street is the one with the transformer." A similar incident occurred when going to pick up a friend at her apartment complex. To let me know how to locate where she lived, she told me her apartment was the one by the third dumpster. That's sprawl! By extreme contrast, to this kind of artless miscellany, Wright envisioned where and how we live to be a large scale work of art, inspired by the regenerative beauty of nature.

What I experienced for more than two decades at Taliesin and Taliesin West were a places where work, education, culture, and entertainment were integrated with localized food production, the conservation of water and energy, and being able to live without the costly back and forth commute between home and work.

Taliesin West as a Living Laboratory

Considering the cultural, educational history of its extraordinary design, its location in the creative atmosphere of the Sonoran Desert, along with the area's attraction and easy accessibility for an international audience, Wright's creation cries out for a new expression.

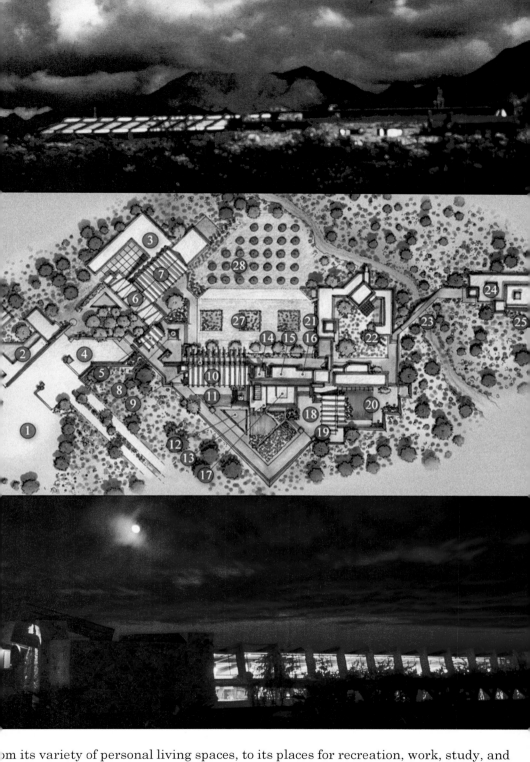

om its variety of personal living spaces, to its places for recreation, work, study, and
ebration, the design of Taliesin West is as orchestrated as a great symphony.

The aerial photo shows a portion of the land surrounding Taliesin West which Wright held in trust for the future. As expressed on the facing page, 75 percent of the land would be left in perpetuity around the historic core. The remaining 25 percent would become a strategic orchestration of related provisions for research, education and international outreach.

I see this new life as an international center that would embrace and be continually updated with the accelerating breakthroughs in technology. It would go further (again quoting E.O. Wilson) to address "what it will take to provide a satisfying and sustainable life for everyone into the indefinite future."

To provide a sense as to how a plan for the future might unfold, there are approximately 470 acres of land surrounding Taliesin West that are owned by the Frank Lloyd Wright Foundation. I have proposed setting aside a historic district consisting of the original structures, along with surrounding open space and protected viewsheds which would account for 75 percent or a little over 350 acres. This would allow the remaining 25 percent or 120 acres to be reserved for the addition of carefully programmed facilities designed to support and further the Foundation's educational mission by way of a wide variety of continually updated, community-centered demonstrations.

This approach would treat the historic district as the "art" and everything else, as a kind of architectural background, not unlike that of nature itself. Anything added would take its respectful place with its focus being on high performance utilization, including innovations for daylighting, energy, and water conservation along with systems that recycle their own wastes. Everything, including new forms of housing would be continuously monitored to document its level of performance and periodically updated as warranted by the on-going experiments. The Taliesin West campus would include greatly expanded visitor-centered exhibits with provisions for all levels of educational programming, and all manner of on-site experimentation. At various times of the year, the public tours that now occur throughout the historic buildings would be expanded to showcase every aspect of the demonstration campus, greatly increasing it's educational experience and outreach.

If ever there was an opportunity to combine the global magnetism of Frank Lloyd Wright, the growing focus of environmental intelligence, and the living demonstration of Taliesin West with the creative atmosphere of the desert southwest along with other cultural attractions of the greater community, this would be its beating heart!

What the 21st Century needs most will not result from more scholarly studies, although they have their place and will surely continue. What is most urgently needed are on-the-ground demonstrations of the power of purpose-centered communities, as exemplified by Frank Lloyd Wright, both by way of his writings and drawings and his own prototypical communities at Taliesin and Taliesin West.

Frank Lloyd Wright demonstrated so much of that which is essential for both humanity and nature. It is time to rekindle and extend that creative spirit. Wright's living example by way of Taliesin West exists for all to see. What doesn't yet exist is the kind of powerful vision for relaunching this global asset in terms that address the challenges and opportunities of the 21st Century. Whatever form that takes, for the good of this and all future generations, may this global treasure be given its rightful place on the world stage.

Mr. and Mrs. Frank Lloyd Wright

AFTERWORD

Jeff Stein

The comprehensive reach of this amazing book, so very different from the business-as-usual norm of the present, inspires two observations. The first observation is that the author's message is made ever-more significant because it comes from a producing architect and planner who has been uncommonly effective within the opportunities and constraints of the here and now.

The second observation is to emphasize why the author felt the need to take on such a comprehensive and global view. This book is the latest in a series that Vern Swaback has written and published during his long and creative career. Each publication has had a message much like the one embedded in these pages:

> Community matters...
> Design matters...
> Here's how.

All reasoned arguments from a visionary designer and thinker who can see how we might still design a rich future for life on earth.

Let me now add an exclamation point to Swaback's insights.

I received a draft manuscript of this book on August 20, 2013. That date marked "Earth Overshoot Day" for the year. Earth Overshoot Day has occurred each year since the 1970's. It is a day on the calendar when "our consumption for the year exceeds Earth's ability to replenish those resources."

This situation, a single species living beyond our means within the finite system that is Earth, is what Swaback is writing about. While the world talks about over-consumption and the existing culture that was designed to induce it, with this book Swaback points to remedies. His argument is about creating global equity and how we can design it by tending to our community – and thus our ecological footprint. Here in the US 5% of the world's population consumes 20% of Earth's resources. If we expect the whole world to live equitably at that same frenetic level of consumption, we will need four earths to support us. Swaback's message is that we can design solutions to this conundrum.

There are difficulties. First, we won't be gifted with four Earth's to support us anytime soon. And beyond that, how many of us want to alter our high-consumption lifestyles? We see wars over scarce resources, read about global economic collapse, the 1% vs 99%, 47 million Americans on food stamps, more than a billion people worldwide living in urban squatters' settlements, more than two billion lacking access to resources required to meet their basic needs.

And so we are in Overshoot. The Global Footprint Network along with the New Economics Foundation are the organizations that mark Earth Overshoot Day. As of mid-August, 2013 humanity had exhausted nature's budget for the year, followed by operating in overdraft, say spokespersons for these organizations. The Global Footprint Network tracks humanity's demand on the planet's ecological resources (such as food provisions, raw materials and carbon dioxide absorption) — its Ecological Footprint — against nature's ability to replenish those resources and absorb waste. Their data show that in less than eight months (in a culture mistakenly designed to do just this) we have used as much nature as our planet can regenerate for the entire year.

The rest of the year corresponds to "Overshoot." Through the fall and winter of 2013 we kept-up an ecological deficit by continuing to deplete stocks of fish, trees and other resources, and accumulate waste such as carbon dioxide in the atmosphere and oceans. The Global Footprint

AFTERWORD

Network puts it this way, "As our level of consumption, or resource budget grows, the interest we are paying on this mounting ecological debt — shrinking forests, biodiversity loss, fisheries collapse, food shortages, degraded land productivity and the build-up of carbon dioxide in our atmosphere and oceans — not only burdens the environment but also undermines our economies. Climate change — a result of greenhouse gases being emitted faster than they can be absorbed by forests and oceans — is the most widespread impact of ecological overspending."

We cannot pretend to produce "qualitative easing" to replicate the resources of the Earth. Life-support resources provided by the Earth are neither expendable nor made of paper. This deficit cannot be "written off" or hidden.

But a solution can be designed. With a crusading architect's response to all of this, Vern Swaback's life-long goal has always been to bring the insights of the specialized few into the mainstream of our daily decision-making. Here is how Neal Pierce of the Washington Post Writers Group, first quoted, then commented on one of Swaback's earlier books, *Designing the Future*:

> "Future power and fortunes will come to those who can demonstrate relationships between privacy and community, between cities and towns, between nations, and ultimately, between humanity and the Earth..." If a capitalist architect-planner is willing to crawl out on that branch, the rest of us might at least consider our routine approaches – whether there isn't a radically higher possibility of who we might be and what we might accomplish with our lives."

Buckminster Fuller said, "On Spaceship Earth there are no passengers, only crew." Vernon Swaback now asks us to understand and accept that as crew we are also all designers, and that it is within our grasp to design our way out of this situation. Begin to think clearly about design issues in your own community. Our individual and collective ability to make a difference is what Frank Lloyd Wright called, "Taking a positive hand in creation". It is a challenge that Vern Swaback asks us to take on in the spirit of "urgent joy".

Jeff Stein
Scottsdale, Arizona

Award-winning architect, writer and educator, Jeff Stein AIA is an architect and president of Cosanti Foundation, the urban research organization founded by Paolo Soleri. He previously taught architecture in the Career Discovery program of the Harvard GSD; headed the department of architecture at Wentworth Institute in Boston; and for seven years he was Dean of the Boston Architectural College. He has taught at architecture schools in the US and at the Technicum Winterthur, Zurich, and Ecole d'Architecture Languedoc-Rousillon, in Montpellier, France. Mr. Stein has written for ARCHITECTURE BOSTON magazine and was for ten years architecture critic for the New England newspaper, BANKER+TRADESMAN. He lectures widely about Arcosanti, energy and urban design, including at the Tel Aviv-Yafo Centennial Conference on Urban Sustainability, in Montreal at the World EcoCities Congress, and at the Santa Fe Institute.

PUTTING IT ALL
TOGETHER

"We who love architecture and recognize it as the great sense of structure in
whatever is music, painting, sculpture, or life itself

– must somehow act as intermediaries

– maybe missionaries."

–Frank Lloyd Wright

As stated on the proceeding page, Wright quite literally saw the practice of architecture as partnering with nature. "Whenever he puts a building upon the earth beneath the sun ... he too, is no less a feature of the landscape than the rocks, trees, bears or bees of that Nature to which he owes his being."[1] It is precisely because our markets don't see things this way that our actions have become a threat to life itself.

Knitting together everything discussed in this book, the unfinished work of Frank Lloyd Wright remains of ever-more critical importance because he exemplified what the present and future of humankind needs most. In his life and work he mastered two related, but very different worlds which Wendell Berry, an award-winning author of more than fifty books portrays as "Two Economies" – "The Great Economy" and the "Little Economy." Berry defines the latter as anything that falls into the category of "factual knowledge, calculations, and manipulation"...a human economy that "can evaluate, distribute, use, and preserve things of value, (but) cannot create value."

Berry goes on to assert that "Value can originate only in the Great Economy. It is true enough that humans can add value to natural things. We may transform trees into boards, and transform boards into chairs, adding value at each transformation. In a good human economy, these transformations would be made by good work, which would be properly valued and the workers properly rewarded. But a good human economy would recognize at the same time that it was dealing all along with materials and powers that it did not make. It did not make trees, and it did not make the intelligence and talents of the human workers. What the humans have added at every step is artificial, made by art, and though the value of art is critical to human life, it is a secondary value." [1]

Fast forward to the 21st Century where our beliefs in "artificial intelligence" extend to, the world-shaping reach "of robotics, infinite computing, ubiquitous broadband networks, digital manufacturing, nanomaterials, synthetic biology, and many other exponentially growing technologies" that will enable us "to make greater gains in the next two decades than we have in the previous two hundred years." We are told that we will soon have the ability "to meet and exceed the basic needs of every man, woman, and child on the planet. Abundance for all is within our grasp." [2]

When everything on the foregoing list of achievements has moved from being excitingly new to taking its place in the annals of human history (as it surely will), it will all still remain in the world that Wendell Berry defines as the "Little Economy". And as we have asked in a prior chapter, would any of these technological accomplishments, on their own, have produced a Shakespeare, Bach, Michelangelo, or Rembrandt? Furthermore will such breakthroughs take humanity beyond the unrealized Utopias of Plato, Thomas, More and others? Or should we simply embrace them for the amazing achievements they represent without forgetting that they exist only in the lesser of our two worlds? Frank Lloyd Wright is revered because he embraced both worlds. In the world of our human behaviors he observed that, "Humans are just a collection of appetites. To the extent that one's appetites are either divine or base, so will be their life experience."

He was a master of the here and now world of the relevant, which he referred to "being true to the time, the place and man." In the other world he might, with good reason, be considered a mystic. He helped us to understand and design in ways that extend far beyond the obvious. In his words, "Whether people are fully conscious of this or not, they actually derive countenance and sustenance from the atmosphere of the things they live in or with. They are rooted in them just as a plant is in the soil in which it is planted."

The Power Of Design

Richard Farson, Ph.D is high among those who have articulated the role of design. He was the founding Dean of the School of Design at the California Institute of the Arts and a 30-year member of the Board of Directors of the International Design Conference in Aspen, where he served as president for seven years. The following observations are from Farson's book, *The Power of Design, A Force for Transforming Everything.*

"I am absolutely in awe of the creativity and courage that designers continually demonstrate. I cannot begin to fathom where they go inside themselves to find such beautiful, imaginative, and functional designs. I so admire their ability to continually put their work and themselves on the line. But more important, I have great respect for their ability to make a better world. Indeed, I've come to think that they represent the profession with the greatest potential to rescue us from the multiple disasters we face and even move us to a new level of humanity. [3] Designers could eventually reduce perhaps all those aspects of our lives that are most troubling: crime, addiction, divorce, physical and mental illness, alcoholism, child abuse, and suicide. The reason other professions cannot make this claim is that the design of environments, situations and experiences is more powerful in eliciting our best than are the practices of any other profession. That's why design should be supported as essential to the public good. It can indeed build a better world." [4]

We Are All Designers

We all know what it is to give our designed best to that which is close to home, including our own houses, neighborhoods, schools, and the environments in which we work, shop and play. It would be difficult, in fact impossible, to have a well-designed experience of one's home, without a well-designed context in which the daily experiences of our life and work take place.

The accelerating changes that will occur in the present century require that these same kinds of mutually supportive relationships extend to the ever-increasing cooperation and competition of the greater community. As we move from the world of design to the design of the world, in addition to the design of houses and buildings may we be stretched, inspired and motivated by these closing words from Richard Farson.

"Designers can foster creativity, community, security, effectiveness, understanding, and affection...Design may soon become the byword of leadership and management. Because of the growing recognition of the designer's power to affect human behavior, increasing numbers and organization specialists think executives should adopt a design perspective. Management guru Tom Peters says it flatly: Everything is design." [5]

In addition to everything being a matter of design, given the dynamics of the 21st century it is time to acknowledge that we are all designers. The more aware we become concerning our human assault on the ecosystems of nature without which we could not exist, the more we are beginning to acknowledge our interdependence with both nature and each other. This will lead to the force of weapons being replaced by the power of ideas, and the doctrines of belief being replaced with the creativity of faith. The result will be a new and growing sense of stewardship and creativity. That which has so easily separated and threatened our very existence, will be replaced with an unprecedented local to global understanding and celebration for the gifts of life.

The Two Worlds Community Foundation

The research, design and publication of this book is an example of the Foundation's design-based, educational outreach. Its public charity status as a 509(a)(2) entity provides for the Foundation to have revenue from exempt services, including seminars and related projects.

Activities recorded on the Foundation's website, are early illustrations of its mission. Additional insights are indicated in the following excerpts from the Foundation's filing with the IRS:

> The Foundation was established to communicate, and cultivate the ecological, technological, behavioral, and economic relationships required for the sustainable design and development of humanity's built environments.

> The term "Two Worlds Community" refers to the two worlds in which we live: The "Operational World" is the one in which we carry out our daily affairs, involving economic markets and financial transactions, political forums, sporting events, entertainment and fashion—a world of "me" in which the commitments and transactions tend to favor our more obvious and near-at-hand interests. The "Sustaining World" consists of the natural ecosystems from which we derive the basic necessities of life as well as the more holistic and "spiritual" dimensions of human existence, including education, science, religion, the arts and culture—a world of "we" in which the nature of our behaviors and commitments tend to be more long-term.

> By initiating and supporting focused exploration, analysis, and modeling of sustainable practices in the design and construction of our built space, the Foundation will address the multiple issues of human habitation in a more integrated way than what has historically resulted from the

combination of standardized codes and ordinances and the daily transactions in the private and public sectors.

The Foundation's vision contemplates the future as a time of unprecedented demand for creativity and service. The Two Worlds Community premise is that there will be a holistically designed future for humanity, or there will be no human future. The Foundation exists to bring together the Operational and Sustaining Worlds into a cohesive community where both interests complement and profit from a coherent system of accounting.

Design shapes both our personal and shared experiences. It is the fundamental integration between the nature we inherit, the technology we invent, and the behaviors we practice. Design is the rudder of culture, marshalling the use of the earth's resources, creating beauty in the physical environment and helping to shape the meaning of life itself. An overview of the Foundation's programs includes:

- Conducting and sponsoring research,
- Publishing newsletters and books consistent with the Foundation's exempt purposes
- Conducting global design competitions
- Organizing seminars and forums for advanced discussions on sustainable development.
- Designing and implementing (or assisting others to implement) pilot projects that address the urgent need for a more informed and long-range approach to the shaping of our built environments.

Looking Back and Forth

The Foundation's website provides an illustrated account of its first urban design competition which attracted interest from all over the world. The winning entries included exceptional proposals from the University of Toronto, Harvard, Qindao University in China and the University of Arizona.

Very different from the global outreach of the first, the second competition was imbedded into the Colleges of Architecture, Planning and Landscape Architecture at the University of Arizona. This was followed by the Navajo Challenge which was open to any Navajo student in good standing at any College or University. This program was designed to inspire young Native Americans to propose new ventures that they would commit to undertake for the benefit of their culture and its people. The winning proposals for these three competitions were presented at Arizona State University, the University of Arizona and at the American Planning Association's 2013 Conference in Scottsdale.

Concurrent with the publication of *Frank Lloyd Wright's Unfinished Work* is the Foundation's next competition, known as "The Ecological Community" which is a 21st century version of the existing intentional communities of the past, including the Taliesin way of life that Frank Lloyd Wright designed for his own life and work. The focus will be on the creation of highly individualized communities for the future all made possible by the digital revolution. In addition to this local to global outreach, the Foundation provides pro bono services to other non-profits and has published six prior books, all as described on the Two Worlds Foundation's website.

Top: The Harvard/University of Toronto team presenting their winning entry to the Foundation's International Sustainable City Competition; Lower Right: The students from Qingdao Technological University in China received the Silver Award.

Individuals wishing to express interest or ask questions concerning this work or to make a tax-deductible contribution may contact the Foundation in any of the following ways:

Website: www.twoworldsfoundation.org
Email: info@twoworldsfoundation.org
Phone: 480.991.1942
Fax: 480.367.2101

Mailing Address:
Two Worlds Community Foundation
7550 East McDonald Drive, Suite A
Scottsdale, Arizona 85250

NOTES

Title Page
E.O. Wilson, *The future of Life*, 2002, page 22.

Introduction

1. Norman Meyers and Jennifer Kent, *The New Gaia Atlas of Planet Management*, 2005, page 8.
2. Ibid., page 10.
3. Ibid., page 22.
4. Frederick Turner, *The Culture of Hope, A New Birth of the Classical Spirit*, 1995, page 233.

Designing the Future

1. Bernard Rudofsky, *Architecture without Architects, an Introduction to Nonpedigreed Architecture*, 1964, page 3.
2. Ibid., page 1.
3. Ibid., Backcover.
4. Bruce Mau and Jennifer Leonard, *Massive Change*, 2004, page 11.

Economics, Science, Art and Religion

1. Stanley Bing, *Fortune: Lessons from the Fall*, September 16, 2013, page 164.
2. Stephen A. Marglin, *The Dismal Science: How Thinking like an Economist Undermines Community*, 2008, page 1.
3. Charles B. Handy, Beyond Certainty: *The Changing Worlds of Organization*, 1996, page 1.
4. Ibid., page 5.
5. Walt Whitman, *Leaves of Grass*, 1895.
6. http://www.opednews.com/kall_070104_hudson_smith.htm, pages 2, 4.

7. Harvey Cox, The Secular City, 1966, page 1.
8. Lloyd Geering, *Christianity Without God*, 2002, page 140.
9. Robert Wright, *The Evolution of God*, 2009, page 3.
10. Ibid., page 376.
11. John Robbins. *Healthy at 100: How You Can - at Any Age –
    Dramatically Increase Your Life Span and Your Health Span*, 2006, page 286.
12. Ibid., page 278.
13. John Steinbeck, *The Log from the Sea of Cortez*, 1951.
14. Robert Wright, *Non-Zero: The Logic of Human Destiny*, 2000, page 331.
15. Manly P. Hall, *Pathways of Psychology*, 1947, page 39.
16. Lloyd Geering, *Christianity Without God*, 2002, pages 223, 224.

From Plato to the Present

1. Kamal Amin, *Excursions: Essays for All Seasons*, 2009, pages 53, 54.

Utopia or Oblivion

1. Buckminster R. Fuller, *Utopia or Oblivion: The Prospects for Humanity*,
   1969, page 1.
2. Ibid., page 2.
3. Lloyd Steven Sieden, *Buckminster Fuller's Universe: His Life and Work*,
   1989, page 87, 88.
4. Ibid., page viii.
5. Buckminster Fuller, *The World Game Handbook*, 1993, pages 16, 17.
6. Rachel Botsman, *What's Mine Is Yours: The Rise of Collaborative
   Consumption*, 2010, page 170, 171.
7. Peter H. and Steven Kotler, *Abundance: The Future Is Better than You
   Think*, 2012, page 120.

Technology and its Limits

1. Rick Smolan and Jennifer Erwit, *The Human Face of Big Data*, 2012, End papers.
2. Buckminster R. Fuller, *Utopia or Oblivion: The Prospects for Humanity*, 1969, page 270.
3. Peter H. Diamandis and Steven Kotler, *Abundance: The Future Is Better than You Think*, 2012, page 11.
4. Ibid., page 193.
5. Thom Hartmann, T*he Last Hours of Ancient Sunlight: The Fate of the World and What We Can Do Before It's Too Late*, 2004, page 2.
6. Rick Smolan and Jennifer Erwit, *The Human Face of Big Data*, 2012, Front End papers.
7. Richard Farson, *The Power of Design: A Force for Transforming Everything*, 2008, page 44.
8. Edward O. Wilson, *The Creation: An Appeal to Save Life on Earth*, 2006, page 10.
9. Mialy Csikszentmihalyi, *Harper Perennial*, 1990.

Ownership and Stewardship

1. Thom Hartmann, *The Last Hours of Ancient Sunlight: The Fate of the World and What We Can Do Before It's Too Late*, 2004, page 1.
2. Norman Meyers and Jennifer Kent, *The New Gaia Atlas of Planet Management*, 2005, page 148.
3. Lester R. Brown, *World on the Edge: How to Prevent Environmental and Economic Collapse*, 2011, page 10.
4. Norman Meyers and Jennifer Kent, *The New Gaia Atlas of Planet Management*, 2005, page 175.
5. Robert Neuwirth, *Shadow Cities: A Billion Squatters, a New Urban World*, pages 285, 286.
6. Ibid., page 286.
7. Ibid., page 290.
8. Aldo Leopold, A *Sand County Almanac*, 1949, page ix.
9. Edward O. Wilson, *The Future of Life*, 2002, pages 157,158.

The Anatomy of Peace

1. Emery Reves, *The Anatomy of Peace*, 1945, 1946, page 29.
2. Václac Havel, *The Art of the Impossible: Politics and Morality in Action*, 1997.
3. George Magnus, *The Age of Aging: How Demographics are Changing with Global Economy and Our World*, 2009, page 237.
4. Norman Meyers and Jennifer Kent, *The New Gaia Atlas of Planet Management*, 2005, page 278.
5. Riane Eisler. *The Chalice and the Blade: Our History, Our Future*, 1987, 1995, pages xiii, xix.
6. Ibid., page 17.
7. Ibid., page 19.
8. Ruth Sivard, *World Military and Social Expenditures*, 1983, page 195.
9. Elizabeth McLeod, I*f Women Ruled the World*, 2011, pages 246, 247.
10. Norman Meyers and Jennifer Kent, *The New Gaia Atlas of Planet Management*, 2005, page 225.
11. Ibid., page 224.

Frank Lloyd Wright's Unfinished Work

1. Bruce Mau and Jennifer Leonard, *Massive Change*, 2004, page 45.
2. http://www.census.gov/prod/cen2010/briefs/c2010br-14.pdf, page 5.
3. George Magnus, *The Age of Aging: How Demographics are Changing with Global Economy and Our World*, 2009, page 304.
4. Ibid, page 303.
5. Paul Kennedy, *Preparing for the 21st Century*, 1994, page 59.
6. Rachel Botsman and Roo Rogers, *What's Mine is Yours: The Rise of Collaborative Consumption*, 2010, Inside front cover.
7. Robert Neuwirth, *Shadow Cities: A Billion Squatters, a New Urban World*, pages 281, 282.
8. Herbert Girardet, *Cities, People, Planets: Livable Cities for a Sustainable World*, 2004, pages 114, 115.
9. Richard Rogers and Philip Gumuchdjlan, *Cities for a Small Planet*, pages 2, 27.

10. George Magnus, *The Age of Aging*, 2009, page 230.
11. Harm de Blij, *Why Geography Matters: Three Challenges Facing America : Climate Change, the Rise of China, and Global Terrorism,* 2005, page 95.
12. George Magnus, *The Age of Aging,* 2009, pages 304, 305.

Surrounded by Miracles

1. http://www.freedomhouse.org/content/our-history
2. Robert Wright, *Non-Zero: The Logic of Human Destiny*, 2000, page 19.
3. Dee Hock, *Birth of the Chaordic Age*, 1999, Frontice Page.
4. Ibid., pages 45, 43.
5. Buckminster Fuller, *Inventory of World Resources Trends and Needs*, 1963.
6. Thom Hartmann, *The Last Hours of Ancient Sunlight: The Fate of the World and What We Can Do Before It's Too Late*, 2004, page 317.
7. Joseph S. Nye, Jr., *The Future of Power*, 2011, page 222.
8. Riane Eisler, *The Chalice and the Blade: Our History, Our Future*, 1987, 1995, page 185.

Putting it all Together

1. Wendell Berry. *What matters? Economics for a Renewed Commonwealth*, 2010, page 116.
2. Peter H. Diamandis and Steven Kotler. *Abundance: The Future is Better than you Think*, 2012, inside cover summary.
3. Richard Farson, *The Power of Design: A Force for Transforming Everything*, 2008, page 1.
4. Ibid., page 30.
5. Ibid., page 33.

BIBLIOGRAPHY

Amin, Kamal. *Excursions: Essays for All Seasons*. Scottsdale: Masry, 2009.

Beatty, Jack, and Peter F. Drucker. *The World According to Peter Drucker*. New York: Free, 1998.

Bellah, Robert Neelly. *Habits of the Heart: Individualism and Commitment in American Life*. Berkeley: University of California, 1985.

Berry, Wendell. *What matters? Economics for a Renewed Commonwealth*, Berkeley Counterpoint 2010.

Block, Peter. *The Answer to How Is Yes: Acting on What Matters*. San Francisco, CA: Berrett-Koehler, 2002.

Botsman, Rachel, and Roo Rogers. *What's Mine Is Yours: The Rise of Collaborative Consumption*. New York: Harper Business, 2010.

Brockman, John, ed. *What Are You So Optimistic About?* New York: Harper Perennial, 2007.

Brown, Lester R. *World on the Edge: How to Prevent Environmental and Economic Collapse*. New York: W.W. Norton, 2011.

Burroughs, James H. *In Praise of Zero; Thoughts on Revealed Religion and Nature,*. Philadelphia: Dorrance, 1964.

Campbell, Joseph, Michael Toms, John M. Maher, and Dennie Briggs. *An Open Life*. New York: Perennial, 1990.

Csikszentmihalyi, Mihaly. *Flow: The Psychology of Optimal Experience*. New York: Harper Perennial, 1990.

Cox, Harvey. *The Future of Faith*. New York: Harper One, 2009.

Cox, Harvey. *The Secular City; Secularization and Urbanization in Theological Perspective*. New York: Macmillan, 1966.

Day, Christopher. *Places of the Soul: Architecture and Environmental Design as a Healing Art*. Oxford [England: Architectural, 2004.

de, Blij, Harm J. *Why Geography Matters: Three Challenges Facing America : Climate Change, the Rise of China, and Global Terrorism*. New York, NY: Oxford UP, 2005.

De Bono, Edward. *I am Right You Are Wrong: From Rock Logic to Water Logic*. New York: Viking, 1990, 1991.

Deloria, Vine. *God is Red: A Native View of Religion*. Golden: Fulcrum Publishing, 2003.

Diamandis, Peter H., and Steven Kotler. *Abundance: The Future Is Better than You Think*. New York: Free Press, 2012.

Ehrenhalt, Alan. *The Lost City: Discovering the Forgotten Virtues of Community in the Chicago of the 1950's*. New York: BasicBooks, 1995.

Einstein, Albert. *The World as I See It*. New York: Citadel Press, 1956.

Ellison, Sheila. *If Women Ruled the World: How to Create the World We Want to Live in: Stories, Ideas, and Inspiration for Change*. Maui, Hawaii: Inner Ocean Publishing, 2004.

Enriquez, Juan. *As the Future Catches You: How Genomics & Other Forces Are Changing Your Life, Work, Health & Wealth*. New York: Crown Business, 2001.

Enriquez, Juan. *The Untied States of America: Polarization, Fracturing, and Our Future*. New York: Crown, 2005

Etzioni, Amitai. *The Spirit of Community: The Reinvention of American Society*. New York: Touchstone, 1993.

Farson, Richard. *The Power of Design: A Force for Transforming Everything*. Norcross, Georgia: Greenway Communications, 2008.

Finkelstein, Israel and Neil Silberman. *The Bible Unearthed: Archaeology's New Vision of Ancient Israel and the Origin of its Sacred Texts*. New York: Simon and Schuster, 2002.

Fox, Mathew. *Original Blessing*. Santa Fe, New Mexico: Bear & Company, 1983.

Freed, Judah. *Global Sense: Awakening Your Personal Power for Democracy and World Peace*. Colorado: Media Visions Press, 2006.

Fry, Douglas P. *Beyond War: The Human Potential for Peace*. New York: Oxford UP, 2007.

Fuller, R. Buckminster. *Nine Chains to the Moon*. Carbondale: Southern Illinois University Press, 1963.

Fuller, R. Buckminster. *Utopia or Oblivion: The Prospects for Humanity*. Toronto: Bantam, 1969.

Gardner, Dan. *Future Babble: Why Expert Predictions Are next to Worthless, and You Can Do Better*. New York, NY: Dutton, 2011.

Gardner, James. *The Intelligent Universe: AI, ET and the Emerging Mind of the Cosmos*. Franklin Lakes, NJ: New Page Books, 2007.

Gardner, John. *Self-Renewal: The Individual and the Innovative Society*. New York: W.W. Norton & Company, 1981.

Gelber, Steven M., and Martin L. Cook. *Saving the Earth: The History of a Middle-class Millenarian Movement*. Berkeley: University of California, 1990.

Geering, Lloyd. *Christianity Without God*. Polebridge Press, 2002.

Girardet, Herbert. *Cities People Planet: Livable Cities for a Sustainable World*. Chichester: John Wiley & Sons Ltd., 2004.

Girardet, Herbert and Mendonca, Miguel. *A Renewable World: Energy, Ecology, Equality – A Report for the World Future Council*. London: Green Books, 2009.

Greene, Brian. The Elegant Universe, Superstrings, Hidden Dimensions, and the Quest for the Ultimate Theory. New York: W.W. Norton & Company, 1999.

Hall, Manly Palmer. *Pathways of Philosophy*. Los Angeles: Philosophical Research Society, 1947.

Handy, Charles B. Beyond Certainty: *The Changing Worlds of Organizations*. Boston: Harvard Business School, 1996.

Handy, Charles B. *The Age of Unreason*. Boston, MA: Harvard Business School, 1989.

Hansen, James. *Storms of My Grandchildren: The Truth About the Coming Climate Catastrophe and Our Last Chance to Save Humanity*. New York: Bloomsbury, 2009.

Hartmann, Thom. *The Last Hours of Ancient Sunlight: The Fate of the World and What We Can Do Before It's Too Late*. New York: Three Rivers Press, 2004.

Hartmann, Thom. *The Prophet's Way: A Guide to Living in the Now*. Rochester, Vermont: Park Street Press, 1997 & 2004.

Hawken, Paul. *Blessed Unrest: How the Largest Movement in the World Came into Being and Why No One Saw It Coming*. New York: Penguin Group, 2007.

Hock, Dee. *Birth of the Chaordic Age*. San Francisco: Berrett-Koehler Publishers, Inc., 1999.

Huxley, Aldous. *The Perrenial Philosphy*. New York: Harper Perennial, 1945.

Jones, Robert. *God, Galileo and Geering: A Faith for the 21st Century*. Santa Rosa, California: Polebridge Press, 2005.

Keller, Suzanne. *Community: Pursuing the Dream, Living the Reality*. Princeton and Oxford: Princeton University Press, 2003.

Kennedy, Paul M. *Preparing for the Twenty-first Century*. New York: Random House, 1993.

Klinenberg, Eric. *Going Solo: The Extraordinary Rise and Surprising Appeal of Living Alone*. New York: Penguin, 2012.

Kotkin, Joel. *The New Geography: How the Digital Revolution is Reshaping the American Landscape*. New York: Random House, 2000.

Kotkin, Joel. *The Next 100 Million: America in 2050*. New York: The Penguin Press, 2010.

Kramer, Mark. *Dispossessed: Life in Our World's Urban Slums*. New York: Orbis, 2009.

Laurent, Clint. *Tomorrow's World: A Look at the Demographic and Socio-Economic Structure of the World in 2032*. Singapore (Asia): John Wiley & Sons, 2013.

Leopold, Aldo. *A Sand County Almanac*. London: Oxford University Press, 1949.

Lima, Antonietta Iolanda. *Soleri: Architecture as Human Ecology*. New York, NY: Monacelli, 2003.

Luce, Edward. *Time to Start Thinking: America in the Age of Descent.* New York: Atlantic Monthly, 2012.

Magnus, George. *The Age of Aging: How Demographics are Changing the Global Economy and Our World.* Singapore: John Wiley and Sons (Asia), 2009.

Marglin, Stephen A. *The Dismal Science: How Thinking like an Economist Undermines Community.* Cambridge, MA: Harvard UP, 2008.

Marks, Robert W., and R. Buckminster Fuller. *The Dymaxion World of Buckminster Fuller.* Garden City, 1968.

Martinson, Tom. *The Atlas of American Architecture: 2000 Years of Architecture, City Planning, Landscape Architecture, and Civil Engineering.* New York: Rizzoli International Publications, Inc., 2009.

Mau, Bruce, Jennifer Leonard, and The Institute Without Boundaries. *Massive Change.* New York: Phaidon, 2004.

McHarg, Ian L. Design with Nature. *Garden City, NY: Published for the American Museum of Natural History,* 1969.

McHarg, Ian L., and Frederick R. Steiner. T*he Essential Ian McHarg: Writings on Design and Nature.* Washington, DC: Island Press, 2006.

McKibben, Bill. *Deep Economy: The Wealth of Communities and the Durable Future.* New York: Times Books, Henry Holt and Company, 2007.

McKibben, Bill. *Hope, Human and Wild: True Stories of Living Lightly on the Earth.* Boston: Little, Brown and Company, 1995.

Meade, Michael. *The World Behind the World: Living at the Ends of Time.* Seattle: Greenfire Press, 2008.

Mumford, Lewis. *The Story of Utopias*. New York: Viking, 1962.

Murray, Charles. *Human Accomplishment, The Pursuit of Excellence in the Arts and Sciences, 800 B.C. to 1950*, New York: Perennial, 2003.

Myers, Norman and Jennifer Kent. *The New Gaia Atlas of Planet Management*. London: Gaia, Books, 2005.

Neuwirth, Robert. *Shadow Cities: A Billion Squatters, a New Urban World*. New York: Routledge, 2005.

Nisbett, Richard E. *The Geography of Thought: How Asian's and Westerners Think Differently... and Why*. New York: Free Press, 2003.

Nye, Jr., Joseph. *The Future of Power*. New York: Public Affairs, 2011.

Orr, David W. *Earth in Mind: On Education, Environment, and the Human Prospect*. Washington, DC: Island, 1994.

Orr, David W. *Ecological Literacy: Education and the Transition to a Postmodern World*. Albany: State University of New York Press, 1992.

Orr, David W. *The Nature of Design: Ecology, Culture, and Human Intention*. New York: Oxford University Press, 2002.

Osbon, Diane K. (Editor). *Reflections on the Art of Living: A Joseph Campbell Companion*. New York: HarperCollins, 1991.

Osler, Sir William. *A Way of Life*. New York: Dover Publications, 1951.

Pallasmaa, Juhani. *The Embodied Image: Imagination and Imagery in Architecture*. Chichester: John Wiley & Sons, 2011.

Pallasmaa, Juhani. *The Thinking Hand: Existential and Embodied Wisdom in Arthitecture*. Chichester, U.K.: Wiley, 2009.

Peck, M. Scott. *The Different Drum: Community-making and Peace.* New York: Simon and Schuster, 1987.

Pérez, Gómez Alberto. *Built upon Love: Architectural Longing after Ethics and Aesthetics.* Cambridge, MA: MIT, 2006.

Pinker, Steven. *The Better Angels of Our Nature: Violence has Declined.* New York: Penguin Books, 2011

Reves, Emery. *The Anatomy of Peace,.* New York: Harper & Bros., 1946.

Ridley, Matt. *The Rational Optimist: How Prosperity Evolves.* New York: Harper, 2010.

Ross, Andrew. *Bird on Fire: Lessons from the Worlds Least Sustainable City.* New York: Oxford University Press, 2011.

Rogers, Richard, and Philip Gumuchdjian. *Cities for a Small Planet.* London: Richard Rogers, 1997.

Rudofsky, Bernard. *Architecture without Architects, an Introduction to Nonpedigreed Architecture.* New York: Museum of Modern Art; Distributed by Doubleday, Garden City, N.Y., 1964.

Rybczynski, Witold. *City Life: Urban Expectations in a New World.* New York: Scribner, 1995.

Sachs, Jeffrey D. *The Edge of Poverty: Economic Possibilities for Our Time.* New York: The Penguin Press, 2005.

Schmidt, Eric, and Jared Cohen. *The New Digital Age: Reshaping the Future of People, Nations and Business.* London: John Murray, 2013.

Schumacher, E. F. *Small Is Beautiful; Economics as If People Mattered.* New York: Harper & Row, 1973.

Sieden, Lloyd Steven. *Buckminster Fuller's Universe: His Life and Work.* Cambridge, Massachusetts: Perseus Publishing, 1989.

Smolan, Rick, and Jennifer Erwitt. *The Human Face of Big Data*. Sausalito, CA: Against All Odds Productions, 2012.

Speth, James G. *Red Sky at Morning: American and the Crisis of the Global Environment*. New Haven and London: Yale University Press, 2004.

Speth, James G. *The Bridge at the Edge of the World: Capitalism, the Environment and Crossing from Crisis to Sustainability*. New Haven: Yale University Press, 2008.

Spong, John Shelby. *A New Christianity for a New World: Why Traditional Faith is Dying and How a New Faith is Being Born*. San Francisco: HarperCollins, 2001.

Swaback, Vernon D. *The Creative Community: Designing for Life*. Victoria, Australia: Image Publishing Group, 2003.

Swaback, Vernon D. *Creating Value: Smart Development and Green Design*. Washington, D.C.: Urban Land Institute, 2007.

Swimme, Brian Thomas and Mary Evelyn Tucker. *Journey of the Universe,* New Haven and London: Yale University Press, 2011.

Taliesin: *Newspaper Columns by Frank Lloyd Wright and the Taliesin Fellowship, 1934-1937*. Carbondale, Illinois: Southern Illinois University Press, 1992.

Thackara, John. *In the Bubble, Designing in a Complex World*. Cambridge, Massachusetts and London: The MIT Press, 2006.

Todd, Nancy Jack, and John. *From Eco-Cities to Living Machines, Principles of Ecological Design*. Berkeley, California: North Atlantic Books, 1993.

Tomalty, Roger, and Aimee Madsen. Cosanti, *The Studios of Paolo Soleri*. Meyer, Arizona: Cosanti, 2012.

Turner, Frederick. *The Culture of Hope, A New Birth of the Classical Spirit*. New York: The Free Press, 1995.

Tzu, Sun. *The Art of War*. New York: Delacorte, 1973.

Unwin, Raymond. *Town Planning in Practice: An Introduction to the Art of Designing Cities and Suburbs*. Princeton and Oxford: Princeton University Press, 1994.

Wann, David, and David Wann. *Reinventing Community: Stories from the Walkways of Cohousing*. Golden, CO: Fulcrum Pub., 2005.

Wilson, Edward O. *The Creation: An Appeal to Save Life on Earth*. New York: W.W. Norton & Company, 2006.

Wilson, Edward O. *The Future of Life*. New York: Alfred A. Knopf, 2002.

Wilson, Edward O. *The Social Conquest of Earth*. New York: Liveright, 2013.

Wright, Frank Lloyd. *An Autobiography*. Petaluma, CA (first published by Duell, Sloan and Pearce), 1943.

Wright, Frank Lloyd. *An American Architecture*. New York: Horizon Press, 1955.

Wright, Frank Lloyd. *The Living City*. New York: Horizon Press, 1958.

Wright, Robert. *Non-Zero: The Logic of Human Destiny*. New York: Pantheon Books, 2000.

Wright, Robert. *The Evolution of God. New York: Little Brown and Company*, 2009.

Wright, Ronald. *A Short History of Progress*. New York: Carroll & Graf Publishers, 2004.

INDEX

Abrahamic Faiths, 26
Abundance, 46
Adam and Eve, 58
AdvancEd, 135
African Pygmies, 26
Alberobella, 17, 18
Alexander the Great, 71
Amarantides, John, 88
Americans, 71
Amin, Kamal, 33, 34
Amu Dar' ya River, 52
Anticoli Corrado, 15
Apollo Program, 115
Architecture without Architects, 10
Aristotle, 35
Arizona, 73, 113
Arizona State Capitol, 88
Around the World in 80 Days, 43
Athens, 82
Ave Verum, 128
Bach, Johann Sebastian, 28, 48, 123, 124
Bartholomew I, 57
Bay of Pigs, 115
Beattles, 137
Beaulieu, Bryan, 97, 98, 99, 101, 102,
        103, 104, 105, 106, 113, 114
Belluschi, Pietro, 8
Berry, Wendell, 151, 152
Bible, 29
Bierce, Ambrose, 53, 54
Bloom, Harold, 128
Brand, Stewart, 42, 46
British Economy, 21
British Isles, 59
Britishers, 71

Broadacre City, 79
Bronowski, Jacob, 130
Buddhism, 24
Burj Khalifa, 75
Butler, Nicholas Murray, 58
Cabrini Green, 12
California Science Center, 104
Campbell, Joseph, 128
Canadian Cities, 92
Capitalism, 59
Casals, Pablo, 130
Chaordic Age, 124
Chardin, Teilhard de, 58, 97, 131
Chautauqua Institution, 30
Chicago, 38
China, 82
Christianity, 24
Christians, 26, 30
Churchill, Winston, 11, 122
Coffin, William Sloane, 30
Colorado River, 52
Columbia University, 58
Columbia's Avery Library, 76
Columbian Exposition, 75
Communism, 40
Confucianism, 24
Cork, 135
Cooper, Alice, 137
Cox, Harvey, 25
Creative Community, 131, 135
Cruise Missiles, 66
Csikszentmihalyi, Mihaly, 49, 50
Darwin, Charles, 67, 132
de Blij, Harm, 92
De Pree, Max, 22

Dharavi, 84

Drucker, Peter, 81

Dublin, 135

Durrant, Will and Ariel, 35

Earth Day, 101, 104

Earth Overshoot Day, 147

East Valley Institute of Technology, 105

Economist, 93

Egypt, 68

Eiffel Tower, 98, 99, 109, 115

Einstein, Albert, 37, 45, 46, 123, 124, 129

Eisenhower, Dwight D., 65

Eisler, Riane, 67, 128, 129

El Paso, Texas, 26

Emerson, Ralph Waldo, 82, 87

Employment, 81, 82

Europe, 94

European Union, 92

Facebook, 52, 111

Fallingwater, 79

Family Formation, 80

Farson, Richard, 55, 153, 154

Fascism, 59

Federalist No. 6, 59

FLLW's Apprentices, 72, 73

Fortune Magazine, 20

Foster, Norman, 76

Founding Fathers, 71

Founding Mothers, 71

France, 59

Freedom House, 123

Friedman, Milton, 67

Fuller, R. Buckminster, 3, 5, 14, 34, 36-40, 42-46, 52, 63, 95, 99, 126, 129, 149

GAIA, 5

Gammage Auditorium, 2, 74

Ganges River, 52

Garden of Eden, 58

Genesis 1:28, 51, 57

George, Henry, 53, 54

German Economy, 21

Germany, 59, 93

Gerring, Lloyd, 25, 31

Ghandhi, Mohandas, 97

Girardet, Herbert, 91, 92

Global Footprint Network, 148

God, 26, 29, 51 54, 57

Gordon, Shep, 137

Great Pyramid, 115

Greeks, 32

Gromley, Ken, 35

Guardians, 33

Guggenheim Museum, 2, 74, 75, 79

Eiffel, Gustave, 98

Hall, Manly Palmer , 31

Hallet, Jean-Pierre, 27

Hamilton, Alexander, 59

Handy, Charles, 20, 21

Hardiman, Thomas, 35

Hartmann, Thomas, 47, 126, 127

Harvard University, 20, 25, 37 41, 127, 134

Havel, Václav, 58, 61

Hawking, Stephen, 29, 61

Herbet, Frank, 129

Hinduism, 24

HIV/AIDS, 66

Hock, Dee, 124, 126

Holmes, Oliver Wendell, 27

Home Depot, 83

Honey Bee, 40

Illinois, 60

Immanuel Baptist Church, 26

Imperial Hotel, 79

India, 82
Indus River, 52
Industrial Revolution, 122
Interstate Highway System, 115
Iraq War, 66
Islam, 24, 26
Israeli Children, 99
Istanbul, 83
Italian Hilltowns, 15
Italian Riviera, 17
Italy, 93
Japanese Economy, 21
Jesus, 24, 26
Judaism, 24
Juliard, 134
Julius Caesar, 71
Kelly, Petra, 36
Keyes, Ken, 134
Kennedy, John F., 115
Kennedy, Paul, 62
Kissinger, Henry, 58, 59, 65
Kotler, Steven, 151,152
Kitty Hawk, 47
Lake Michigan, 38
Lanik, 109
Laotze, 79
Le Corbusier, 116
Leopold, Aldo, 53, 54, 56
Liberia, 135
Lockheed Martin, 101
London, 91, 92, 135
Lord's Prayer, 27
Los Angeles, 92, 101, 103
Lucas, George, 129
Luke 12:48, 138
Magnus, George, 92
Man in the Maze, 114
Manhattan, 82

Marglin, Stephen A., 20
Marin County, 2, 74
Mau, Bruce, 76, 77
Mayans, 52
McCarty, Steve, 134, 138
McCarty, Trisha, 132-137
McGill University, 55
McHarg, Ian L., 6
McLeod, Elizabeth, 69
McLuhan, Marshall, 55
McVeigh, Timothy, 103
Mead, Margaret, 35
Mesa, Arizona, 105
Mexico City, 56, 135
Meyer, Philippe, 19
Meyers, Norman, 71
Michelangelo, 28, 123, 124
Michigan State University, 92
Microsoft, 117
Middle Ages, 32
Mile High Building, 75
Military Conflicts, 66, 69
Miller, Henry, 119
MIT, 20
Monroe Doctrine, 59
Montague, Ashley, 67
Moore's Law, 46, 47, 48
More, Thomas, 48, 152
Moscow, 59
Mozart, 128
Mrs. Frank Lloyd Wright, 74, 88
Muir, John, 19
Mumbai, 45, 83
Murray, Charles, 120
Museum of Modern Art, 9, 10, 12, 76
Muslims, 26
Nairobi, 83

Napoleon, 71
NASA, 105, 115
National Service Foundation, 103
Neolithic Goddess Worship, 68
Netherlands, 93
Neuwirth, Robert, 54, 83
Nevada, 114
New York, 30, 43, 74, 79, 116, 142
New York Times, 82
Newton, Sir Isaac, 37
Niemeyer, Oscar, 116
Nine Chains to the Moon, 43
North Central, 135
Notre Dame, 115
Nye, Joseph S., 127
Ogallala Aquifer, 52
Oklahoma Federal Building, 103
Olmsted, Frederick Law, 123, 124
Origin of Inequality, 53
Oxford, 20, 135
Palestinian Children, 99
Panama Canal, 103
Paris World's Fair, 98
Peloponnesian War, 32
Pfeiffer, Bruce Brooks, 88
Phoenix, Arizona, 117
Pierce, Neal, 149
Plato's Republic, 32, 35, 152
Positano, 15, 16
Preparing for the Twenty-First Century, 62
Princeton, 25
Progress and Poverty, 53
Pruitt Iqoe, 12
Public Art, 23
Quixote, Don, 115, 116
Reclus, Élisée, 98
Religion, 28, 59
Rembrandt, 48

Renaissance, 32
Reves, Emery, 58, 59, 60, 61, 65, 70
Rice University, 115
Rio de Janeiro, 83
Rio Grande River, 52
Ritz Carlton, 135
Robbins, John, 26, 27
Rockefeller, John D., 116
Rogers, Richard, 76
Rome, 15, 82
Rousseau, Jean-Jacques, 53, 54
Rudofsky, Bernard, 10, 12, 15
Sabine Mountains, 15
Saarinen, Eero, 8
Sand County Almanac, 54
Satan, 26
Schmidt, Eric, 47
Schwartz, Bob, 35
Schweitzer, Albert, 26
Seven Deadly Sins, 47
Shakespeare, William, 48, 55, 128
Shaw, George Bernard, 30, 116
Shell Oil Company, 20
Sivard, Ruth, 69
Slumdog Millionaire, 84
Smith, Adam, 20, 21, 53, 54
Smith, Huston, 24
Smith, Stephanie, 41
Smithsonian Castle, 101
Smithsonian Institution, 103
Socialism, 59
Socrates, 8, 35
Solomon, 55
Spain, 93
Squatter Cities, 83, 84
St. Croix, 103
St. John, 103
St. Thomas, 103, 105

Stalin, 71

Stanford-trained, 42

StarShine Academy, 131, 133-137

Stein, Jeff, 147-150

Steinbeck, John, 28

Steiner, Frederick, 2-4

Stone Age, 67

Stonehenge, 113, 115

Sudan, 135

Sumerians , 52

Swaback, Caroline, 137

Swaback Partners, 130

Taliesin, 36, 41-43, 57, 73, 74, 77, 86, 88,
    95, 131, 139, 140, 142, 146, 157

Taliesin Fellowship, 74

Taliesin Festival of Music and Dance, 88

Taliesin West, 41, 74, 77, 95, 138-
    146, 151, 152

Tarrytown Institute, 35

Taylor, Elizabeth, 43

Tennyson, Alfred Lord, 96

The American Dilemma, 62

The Anatomy of Peace, 58, 60, 64, 70

The Ecological Community, 157

The Great Globe, 98, 103, 105, 109,
    111-116

Thomas More's Utopia, 32, 34

Thomas, Clarence, 35

Todd, Mike, 43

Tohono O'odham, 114, 115

Tokyo's Kanto Earthquake, 79

U.S. Bureau of Land Management, 114

United Children of Earth, 97, 116

United Kingdom, 93

United Nations, 70, 116

United States, 32, 59, 66, 71, 76, 113

United States Constitution, 71

University of Chicago, 49

University of Minnesota, 98, 101, 110

University of Pennsylvania, 4, 25

University of Texas at Austin, 3

USGS, 114

Utopia or Oblivion, 34, 36, 63, 64

Val di FaFora, 17

Van der Post, Laurens, 32

VISA, 125

Wagner, Richard, 30

Wall Street, 19

Walton, Melani, 134, 136

Washington D.C., 110

Washington monuments, 103

Washington Post, 149

West Bank, 99

West Indies, 103

What's Mine is Yours, 82

White, William H., 119

Whiteman Hall, 141

Whitman, Walt, 23

Whole Earth Catalog, 42

Wilson, Edward O., 57, 67

Wisconsin, 60, 73

World Game, 40

World Game Institute, 41

World Resources Inventory, 39, 40

World Trade Center, 12

World War I, 59, 103

World War II, 64, 122

Wright Brothers, 47

Wright, Frank Lloyd, 5-8, 29, 35, 36, 42,
    43, 67, 73-81, 86, 88-96, 124, 130
    134, 138-146, 141, 151, 152

Wright, Mrs. FLLW, 74, 88, 146

Wright, Robert, 25, 26, 123

Yamasaki, Minoru, 12

Yellow River, 52

Zuckerberg, Mark, 52

Vernon Swaback began his education at the University of Illinois before becoming Frank Lloyd Wright's youngest apprentice. He later served as Director of Planning for Taliesin Associated Architects and Director of the Art and Philosophy of Frank Lloyd Wright at the Frank Lloyd Wright School of Architecture. In 1978 he founded what is today Swaback Partners. In 2005 he became Chairman of the Frank Lloyd Wright Foundation and in 2010 founded the non-profit Two World's Community Foundation. He has been inducted into the College of Fellows by both the American Institute of Architects and The American Institute of Certified Planners.

Photo credits:

Top: Marvin Koner
Bottom: Cassandra Tomei